Haiti's 1994 Ope
Democracy: Mea
Successes and F

Copyright Page

TITLE: Haiti's 1994 Operation Uphold Democracy: Measuring Successes and Failures

1ST Edition

Copyright @ 2023

ISBN: 9798223610199

Table of Contents

Haiti's 1994 Operation Uphold Democracy: Measuring Successes and Failures

By Roberto Miguel Rodriguez

Chapter 1: Operation Uphold Democracy: The 1994 U.S.-led Multinational Military Intervention in Haiti

The Background and Justification for the Intervention

Introduction:

The 1994 U.S.-led multinational military intervention in Haiti, known as Operation Uphold Democracy, was a significant event in both the political history of Haiti and the international community's response to regional conflicts. This subchapter delves into the background and justification for the intervention, providing historians with valuable insights into the reasons behind this military action and its implications.

Historical Context:

To understand the intervention, it is crucial to examine the political history of Haiti before and after the U.S.-led operation. Haiti had long been plagued by political instability, corruption, and human rights abuses. The subchapter explores these issues, shedding light on the dire circumstances that necessitated external intervention.

Role of the United Nations:

The United Nations' involvement in Operation Uphold Democracy was instrumental in providing legitimacy and international support to the intervention. Historians will gain an understanding of the UN's role in coordinating and overseeing the mission, as well as its impact on the operation's overall success.

Impact on Haitian Society and Economy:

Operation Uphold Democracy had profound implications for Haitian society and economy. Historians will explore the short-term and long-term effects of the intervention, including the stabilization of political institutions, economic revitalization, and improvements in human rights and social welfare.

International Response and Diplomatic Implications:

The subchapter examines how the international community reacted to the military intervention and the diplomatic implications it had on regional politics. Historians will gain insights into the various countries' positions and the consequences of their involvement or non-involvement in the operation.

Military Strategy and Tactics:

Analyzing the military strategy and tactics employed during Operation Uphold Democracy provides historians with a comprehensive understanding of the intervention's execution. The subchapter delves into the decision-making process, the use of force, and the military's overall effectiveness in achieving the operation's objectives.

Humanitarian Aspects:

The humanitarian aspects of the intervention, including relief efforts and aid distribution, are crucial when assessing the overall impact of Operation Uphold Democracy. Historians will explore how humanitarian aid was provided, the challenges faced, and the effectiveness of these efforts in mitigating the crisis and improving the lives of Haitian civilians.

Perspectives of Haitian Civilians:

By examining the experiences and perspectives of Haitian civilians during and after Operation Uphold Democracy, historians gain valuable insights into the impact of the intervention on the local population. Their accounts provide a nuanced understanding of the intervention's effects on daily life, social dynamics, and public sentiment.

Assessment of Success or Failure:

The subchapter evaluates the success or failure of Operation Uphold Democracy in achieving its objectives. Historians will critically analyze the operation's outcomes, considering factors such as political stability, the establishment of democratic institutions, and the long-term impact on Haiti's governance.

Media Coverage and Public Perception:

The media coverage and public perception of Operation Uphold Democracy, both domestically and internationally, shaped public opinion and influenced the intervention's legacy. Historians will examine the media narratives, biases, and the public's response to better understand how the intervention was portrayed and understood by different audiences.

Long-Term Consequences and Legacy:

Finally, historians will explore the long-term consequences and legacy of Operation Uphold Democracy on Haiti's political stability and democratic institutions. This subchapter assesses whether the intervention successfully laid the groundwork for lasting change or if it had unintended consequences that hindered Haiti's progress.

Conclusion:

This subchapter offers historians a comprehensive analysis of the background and justification for the intervention, shedding light on its historical context, military and diplomatic strategies, humanitarian aspects, and long-term consequences. By studying these aspects, historians can gain a deeper understanding of Operation Uphold Democracy's impact on Haiti and its significance in the broader field of international interventions.

The Objectives and Goals of Operation Uphold Democracy

Operation Uphold Democracy, the 1994 U.S.-led multinational military intervention in Haiti, was undertaken with a set of specific objectives and goals. These objectives aimed to address the political instability and human rights violations that plagued Haiti before the intervention and to restore democratic governance in the country. This subchapter will delve into the objectives and goals of Operation Uphold Democracy, shedding light on the motivations behind the intervention and its intended outcomes.

One of the primary objectives of Operation Uphold Democracy was to reinstate Jean-Bertrand Aristide as the democratically elected president of Haiti. Aristide, who had been ousted in a military coup in 1991, enjoyed significant popular support, and his return to power was seen as essential for the restoration of democracy in Haiti. The intervention sought to remove the military junta that had taken control and to facilitate Aristide's return.

Another important goal of the intervention was to establish a stable and secure environment in Haiti. The military junta that had seized power in 1991 had unleashed a wave of violence and human rights abuses, leading to a deteriorating security situation. Operation Uphold Democracy aimed to disarm the paramilitary groups and restore law and order in the country, allowing for the safe return of refugees and the provision of humanitarian aid.

Furthermore, Operation Uphold Democracy sought to address the economic challenges faced by Haiti. The intervention aimed to revitalize the Haitian economy through the promotion of foreign investment and the implementation of economic reforms. The goal was to create a foundation for sustainable development and to improve living conditions for the Haitian population.

Lastly, the intervention had broader implications in terms of regional stability and U.S. foreign policy interests. Operation Uphold Democracy aimed to prevent Haiti's political instability from spreading to neighboring countries, which could have had negative consequences for the security and stability of the region. Additionally, the intervention sought to demonstrate the United States' commitment to democratic values and human rights, aligning with its broader foreign policy objectives.

By understanding the objectives and goals of Operation Uphold Democracy, historians can better analyze and assess the success or failure of the intervention in achieving its intended outcomes. This subchapter will provide a comprehensive overview of these objectives, shedding light on the motivations behind the intervention and its impact on Haiti's political stability, democratic institutions, and society at large.

The Key Players and Decision-makers Involved in the Intervention

In order to understand the complexities and dynamics of Operation Uphold Democracy, it is crucial to examine the key players and decision-makers involved in the intervention. This chapter aims to shed light on the individuals and organizations that played pivotal roles in shaping the course and outcomes of this U.S.-led multinational military operation.

At the forefront of the intervention was the United States, which took the lead in organizing and executing Operation Uphold Democracy. President Bill Clinton, along with his advisors, played a crucial role in the decision-making process. Their aim was to restore stability and democracy in Haiti, following the removal of President Jean-Bertrand Aristide in a military coup.

The United Nations also played a significant role in Operation Uphold Democracy. Under the leadership of Boutros Boutros-Ghali, the UN Secretary-General at the time, the organization provided diplomatic support, logistical assistance, and peacekeeping forces to ensure the success of the intervention. The involvement of the UN showcased the international community's commitment to upholding democratic principles and preventing further human rights abuses in Haiti.

Within Haiti, several key figures emerged during the intervention. General Raoul Cédras, who led the military junta responsible for Aristide's removal, became a central figure in the negotiations and discussions surrounding the intervention. On the other hand, President Aristide, who was restored to power following the intervention, played a crucial role in shaping Haiti's political landscape during this period.

Furthermore, the military strategy and tactics employed during the intervention were orchestrated by General Hugh Shelton, who served as the Commander-in-Chief of the U.S. Southern Command. His leadership and decision-making skills were instrumental in ensuring the success of the military operation.

In addition to the key political and military figures, numerous humanitarian organizations and relief efforts were involved in providing assistance to the Haitian people during and after the intervention. These organizations, including the International Red Cross and various non-governmental organizations, played a vital role in delivering aid and rebuilding Haitian society and economy.

Understanding the roles and perspectives of these key players and decision-makers is crucial in assessing the success or failure of Operation Uphold Democracy. By analyzing their actions and motivations, historians can gain a comprehensive understanding of the intervention's impact on Haiti's political stability, democratic institutions, and the long-term consequences it had on the nation.

The Timeline of Events Leading up to the Intervention

The U.S.-led multinational military intervention in Haiti, known as Operation Uphold Democracy, was the result of a series of events that unfolded over several years. To understand the context and significance of the intervention, it is crucial to examine the timeline of events leading up to it.

In the political history of Haiti before the intervention, the country experienced a tumultuous period marked by political instability, corruption, and human rights abuses. The 1991 coup d'état, led by General Raoul Cédras, overthrew President Jean-Bertrand Aristide, a democratically elected leader. This event triggered a wave of violence and repression, forcing thousands of Haitians to flee the country.

The international response to the crisis was mixed. While the United States initially imposed an economic embargo on Haiti, diplomatic efforts to resolve the conflict proved ineffective. As the situation in Haiti deteriorated, with reports of widespread human rights violations and a growing number of refugees, the need for a more decisive action became evident.

In 1994, the United Nations Security Council authorized the use of force to restore democracy in Haiti. Under U.S. leadership, a multinational coalition was formed to carry out the intervention. Operation Uphold Democracy aimed to reinstate President Aristide, disarm paramilitary groups, and provide humanitarian assistance to the Haitian people.

The military strategy employed during the intervention involved a combination of airstrikes, amphibious landings, and ground operations. The multinational force faced significant challenges, including the need to navigate complex political dynamics and maintain the support of the Haitian population.

While the intervention succeeded in achieving its immediate objectives, including the restoration of President Aristide and the disarming of paramilitary groups, its long-term impact on Haitian society and economy was mixed. Despite initial improvements, Haiti continued to face significant challenges, including poverty, political corruption, and institutional weaknesses.

The humanitarian aspects of the intervention were crucial in providing relief efforts and aid distribution to the Haitian people. International organizations and NGOs played a vital role in delivering essential services, such as healthcare, food, and shelter, to those affected by the conflict.

The media coverage and public perception of the intervention, both domestically and internationally, were diverse. While some praised the intervention as a necessary step towards restoring democracy and human rights in Haiti, others criticized it as an example of foreign interventionism.

The long-term consequences and legacy of Operation Uphold Democracy on Haiti's political stability and democratic institutions are subjects of ongoing debate. While the intervention succeeded in reinstating President Aristide, it did not address the underlying structural issues that contributed to Haiti's political instability. The country continues to grapple with challenges related to poverty, corruption, and weak governance.

In conclusion, the timeline of events leading up to the intervention in Haiti provides a comprehensive understanding of the context and significance of Operation Uphold Democracy. By examining the political history, international response, military strategy, humanitarian aspects, and long-term consequences, historians can evaluate the success or failure of the intervention in achieving its objectives and assess its impact on Haiti's society and economy.

The Preparations and Logistics for Operation Uphold Democracy

The success or failure of any military intervention greatly depends on the preparations and logistics that go into it. Operation Uphold Democracy, the 1994 U.S.-led multinational military intervention in Haiti, was no exception. This subchapter delves into the intricate details of the preparations and logistics behind this significant historical event.

Before the intervention could take place, extensive planning was required. The United States, as the leading force, had to coordinate with other participating nations and gather intelligence on the situation in Haiti. This involved assessing the political history of Haiti, both before and after the U.S.-led intervention, to better understand the complexities of the country's internal dynamics.

The role of the United Nations (UN) in Operation Uphold Democracy cannot be overlooked. The UN played a crucial role in supporting and facilitating the intervention, providing logistical support, and ensuring the smooth operation of relief efforts and aid distribution.

The military strategy and tactics employed during Operation Uphold Democracy were carefully crafted to achieve specific objectives. A combination of air and ground operations was utilized to restore stability and democracy in Haiti. The subchapter explores these strategies in detail, shedding light on their effectiveness and impact.

Furthermore, the humanitarian aspects of the intervention are examined, including the relief efforts and aid distribution that took place during and after the operation. This includes the experiences and perspectives of Haitian civilians, who were directly affected by the intervention. Their voices provide valuable insights into the broader impact on Haitian society and economy.

The international response and diplomatic implications of Operation Uphold Democracy are also analyzed. The intervention had far-reaching consequences, both politically and diplomatically, and this subchapter explores the various dimensions of these implications.

Media coverage and public perception played a significant role in shaping the narrative around Operation Uphold Democracy. The subchapter investigates domestic and international media coverage, providing an assessment of how the intervention was portrayed and how public perception evolved over time.

Finally, the long-term consequences and legacy of Operation Uphold Democracy on Haiti's political stability and democratic institutions are critically evaluated. By examining the lasting impact, historians can gain a comprehensive understanding of the intervention's success or failure in achieving its objectives.

In summary, this subchapter on the preparations and logistics for Operation Uphold Democracy provides historians with a detailed account of the planning, coordination, and execution of the intervention. By exploring the various aspects mentioned above, a comprehensive assessment of the intervention's success or failure can be made, contributing to a deeper understanding of this pivotal moment in history.

Chapter 2: The Political History of Haiti before and after the U.S.-led Intervention

The Roots of Political Instability in Haiti

Haiti, a small Caribbean nation that shares the island of Hispaniola with the Dominican Republic, has a long history of political instability. This subchapter aims to explore the roots of this instability, shedding light on the factors that contributed to the need for a U.S.-led multinational military intervention in 1994, known as Operation Uphold Democracy.

To understand the political history of Haiti before and after the U.S.-led intervention, it is crucial to examine the country's turbulent past. From its independence in 1804, Haiti faced numerous challenges such as a weak institutional framework, corrupt political leaders, and a highly unequal society. These factors, combined with a legacy of autocratic regimes and economic mismanagement, created a breeding ground for political instability.

The United Nations played a significant role in Operation Uphold Democracy, providing legitimacy and support to the intervention. By overseeing the transition from military to civilian rule, the UN aimed to restore stability and democratic governance in Haiti. However, the impact of Operation Uphold Democracy on Haitian society and economy was complex. While it brought immediate relief and aid distribution, the long-term consequences on the country's institutions and political stability were mixed.

Examining the international response and diplomatic implications of the intervention is crucial to understanding its broader implications. While some countries supported the intervention as a necessary step to restore democracy, others questioned the motives and methods employed by the United States. This led to debates about sovereignty, interventionism, and the role of foreign powers in nation-building.

The military strategy and tactics employed during Operation Uphold Democracy also influenced its outcome. By combining military force with diplomacy, the intervention sought to minimize casualties while achieving its objectives. However, the experiences and perspectives of Haitian civilians during and after the intervention provide important insights into the human cost of such operations.

Assessing the success or failure of Operation Uphold Democracy is a complex task. While it succeeded in restoring a semblance of democratic governance, challenges such as poverty, corruption, and crime persisted. The media coverage and public perception of the intervention, both domestically and internationally, played a crucial role in shaping its legacy.

Ultimately, the long-term consequences of Operation Uphold Democracy on Haiti's political stability and democratic institutions are still debated today. While the intervention brought temporary stability, its impact on Haiti's long-term development remains a subject of scrutiny. Understanding the roots of political instability in Haiti is crucial to learning from history and ensuring a more stable future for the country.

The Rise and Fall of Jean-Claude "Baby Doc" Duvalier

Jean-Claude Duvalier, commonly known as "Baby Doc," ascended to power in Haiti at the tender age of 19 following the death of his father, François "Papa Doc" Duvalier, in 1971. This marked the beginning of a tumultuous period in Haitian history that would ultimately lead to Baby Doc's own downfall.

Under Baby Doc's rule, Haiti experienced a continuation of the authoritarian regime established by his father. The Duvalier family's brutal Tonton Macoutes paramilitary force maintained a stranglehold on power, suppressing dissent and perpetuating human rights abuses. However, Baby Doc's reign was marked by a degree of relative economic stability compared to his father's tumultuous tenure.

Despite this stability, the lavish lifestyles of the Duvalier family and their cronies contrasted starkly with the dire poverty experienced by the majority of Haitians. Corruption and economic mismanagement further exacerbated the country's social and economic inequalities.

As discontent within Haiti grew, so did international pressure to address the country's human rights abuses and lack of democracy. In 1986, facing mounting opposition and growing unrest, Baby Doc was forced into exile in France. The fall of the Duvalier regime marked a turning point in Haiti's political history, but the country's troubles were far from over.

Following Baby Doc's departure, Haiti experienced a period of political instability and violence. Multiple military coups and a series of weak civilian governments further undermined Haiti's democratic institutions. The international community, particularly the United States, recognized the need for intervention to restore stability and democracy in the country.

Operation Uphold Democracy, a U.S.-led multinational military intervention, commenced in 1994 with the aim of removing the military junta and reinstating Jean-Bertrand Aristide, the democratically elected president. While the operation succeeded in achieving its immediate objectives, the long-term consequences and legacy of Operation Uphold Democracy on Haiti's political stability and democratic institutions remain a subject of debate.

The rise and fall of Baby Doc Duvalier serves as a cautionary tale of the dangers of authoritarian rule and the challenges faced by a country striving to establish a stable democracy. Understanding this chapter in Haiti's history is crucial for historians seeking to analyze the impact of Operation Uphold Democracy and its role in shaping Haiti's political landscape. By examining the rise and fall of Baby Doc, we can gain valuable insights into the complex dynamics of power, democracy, and intervention in Haiti.

The Transition to Democracy and the Presidency of Jean-Bertrand Aristide

As historians delve into the complex history of Operation Uphold Democracy, a significant chapter that cannot be disregarded is the transition to democracy and the presidency of Jean-Bertrand Aristide. This subchapter explores the tumultuous period leading up to Aristide's election, his presidency, and the subsequent impact on Haiti's political stability and democratic institutions.

Before the U.S.-led intervention, Haiti had a long history of political instability, authoritarian rule, and human rights abuses. Operation Uphold Democracy aimed to restore democracy and promote stability in the country. With the support of the international community, including the United Nations, elections were held in 1990, resulting in the historic election of Jean-Bertrand Aristide, a charismatic and popular figure among the Haitian population.

Aristide's presidency, however, was marked by controversy and challenges. He faced opposition from various factions within Haiti, including the military and the elite. The subchapter explores the political struggles, attempted coups, and the eventual removal of Aristide from power in 1991. It also delves into the international response to these events and the diplomatic implications of the intervention.

Despite the challenges, Operation Uphold Democracy played a crucial role in restoring Aristide to power in 1994. The subchapter examines the military strategy and tactics employed during this phase of the operation, highlighting the role of the U.S.-led multinational forces in achieving this objective.

Furthermore, the subchapter delves into the humanitarian aspects of the intervention, including relief efforts and aid distribution. It provides insights into the experiences and perspectives of Haitian civilians during and after Operation Uphold Democracy, shedding light on their hopes, frustrations, and aspirations for a democratic Haiti.

Ultimately, the subchapter evaluates the success or failure of Operation Uphold Democracy in achieving its objectives. It assesses the impact of the intervention on Haitian society and economy, discussing the long-term consequences and legacy on Haiti's political stability and democratic institutions. Additionally, it analyzes the media coverage and public perception of the intervention, both domestically and internationally.

In conclusion, the transition to democracy and the presidency of Jean-Bertrand Aristide is a crucial element in understanding the multifaceted Operation Uphold Democracy. This subchapter provides historians with a comprehensive analysis of the events, challenges, and implications of this period, shedding light on the complex dynamics that shaped Haiti's political landscape.

The Impact of Operation Uphold Democracy on Haitian Politics

Operation Uphold Democracy, the 1994 U.S.-led multinational military intervention in Haiti, had a significant impact on the political landscape of the country. This subchapter aims to explore the consequences of the operation on Haitian politics, shedding light on the challenges and changes faced by the nation's democratic institutions.

Before delving into the impact of Operation Uphold Democracy, it is crucial to understand the political history of Haiti. The country had experienced a turbulent past, marked by political instability, dictatorships, and coups. The intervention aimed to restore democracy and stability by removing the military junta that had overthrown President Jean-Bertrand Aristide.

The role of the United Nations in Operation Uphold Democracy cannot be overlooked. The UN provided crucial support in terms of peacekeeping and facilitating the transition to democracy. Their presence helped maintain stability during the turbulent period of political transition.

Operation Uphold Democracy had far-reaching effects on Haitian society and the economy. The intervention brought relief efforts and aid distribution to the forefront, addressing the urgent needs of the population. However, the long-term impact on the economy was mixed, with some sectors benefiting from increased stability, while others struggled to recover.

The international response and diplomatic implications of the intervention were significant. The operation garnered support from many countries, demonstrating the global commitment to democracy and human rights. However, it also raised questions about sovereignty and the limits of intervention in the internal affairs of a nation.

The experiences and perspectives of Haitian civilians during and after Operation Uphold Democracy provide valuable insights into the successes and failures of the intervention. Their voices shed light on the challenges faced by the local population and the effectiveness of the mission in achieving its objectives.

Assessing the success or failure of Operation Uphold Democracy in achieving its objectives is a complex task. While the intervention succeeded in restoring Aristide to power and establishing a democratic government, challenges persisted, such as corruption, poverty, and political instability.

The media coverage and public perception of the intervention played a crucial role in shaping domestic and international opinions. The portrayal of the operation influenced public support and perception of the mission's effectiveness.

Finally, the long-term consequences and legacy of Operation Uphold Democracy on Haiti's political stability and democratic institutions must be examined. Did the intervention pave the way for lasting democratic governance, or did it merely delay the inevitable challenges that Haiti faced?

In conclusion, Operation Uphold Democracy had a profound impact on Haitian politics. It brought stability, restored democracy, and addressed urgent humanitarian needs. However, the long-term effects on the economy and political stability remain complex, and the assessment of success or failure requires a nuanced understanding of the challenges faced by Haiti before, during, and after the intervention.

Challenges in Establishing Stable Democratic Institutions

In the aftermath of Operation Uphold Democracy, the establishment of stable democratic institutions in Haiti proved to be a formidable challenge. Despite the initial objectives of the intervention being centered around promoting democracy and restoring political stability, the realities on the ground presented numerous hurdles that hindered progress.

One of the key challenges was the deeply ingrained history of political instability in Haiti. Prior to the U.S.-led intervention, Haiti had experienced decades of autocratic rule, coups, and political violence. This tumultuous political history created a culture of distrust and uncertainty among the population, making it difficult to build the foundations of a stable democracy.

Furthermore, the intervention itself faced internal challenges that impacted the establishment of democratic institutions. The role of the United Nations in Operation Uphold Democracy was crucial, but coordinating the efforts of multiple nations and organizations proved complex. Different agendas, priorities, and approaches to governance made it difficult to achieve a unified and cohesive strategy for nation-building in Haiti.

The impact of Operation Uphold Democracy on Haitian society and economy also presented significant challenges. The intervention brought about a temporary halt to the rampant violence and human rights abuses, but it failed to address the underlying socio-economic issues that plagued the country. Poverty, corruption, and lack of infrastructure continued to hinder progress towards stable institutions.

Moreover, the experiences and perspectives of Haitian civilians during and after Operation Uphold Democracy played a crucial role in shaping the challenges faced in establishing democratic institutions. Many Haitians felt alienated and excluded from the decision-making process, leading to a sense of resentment and skepticism towards the intervention. This lack of buy-in from the local population made it difficult to garner support for democratic initiatives and hindered the long-term sustainability of these institutions.

The media coverage and public perception of the intervention, both domestically and internationally, also had a significant impact on the establishment of stable democratic institutions. While the international community initially hailed Operation Uphold Democracy as a success, there were mounting concerns about the extent of the intervention's achievements. Criticisms of heavy-handed tactics and questions about the true intentions of the intervention further complicated efforts to build trust and legitimacy in the democratic process.

Despite these challenges, it is essential to assess the success or failure of Operation Uphold Democracy in achieving its objectives. By critically examining the long-term consequences and legacy of the intervention, historians can provide valuable insights into the impact on Haiti's political stability and democratic institutions. Through a comprehensive analysis of the diplomatic implications, military strategy, humanitarian efforts, and the experiences of Haitian civilians, a nuanced understanding of the challenges faced in establishing stable democratic institutions can be gained. Only by learning from these challenges can future interventions strive for greater success in achieving their objectives and promoting sustainable democratic governance.

Chapter 3: The Role of the United Nations in Operation Uphold Democracy

The Mandate and Involvement of the United Nations in the Intervention

The United Nations played a crucial role in Operation Uphold Democracy, the 1994 U.S.-led multinational military intervention in Haiti. As an international organization dedicated to maintaining peace and security, the United Nations was called upon to help restore stability and democratic governance in Haiti. Under the mandate of UN Security Council Resolution 940, a multinational force was authorized to use all necessary means to facilitate the departure of the de facto regime and support the peaceful transition to a democratically elected government.

The United Nations' involvement in Operation Uphold Democracy was multifaceted. First and foremost, the organization provided the legal and diplomatic framework for the intervention. The Security Council resolution, supported by the international community, gave legitimacy to the military action and underscored the collective commitment to upholding democratic principles.

Additionally, the United Nations played a crucial logistical role in coordinating the multinational force. The organization facilitated the deployment of troops from various countries, ensuring a unified and coordinated approach to the intervention. This coordination was essential to the success of the operation, as it allowed for efficient use of resources and minimized the risk of conflicts among the participating forces.

Furthermore, the United Nations provided a platform for dialogue and diplomacy throughout the intervention. It actively engaged with Haitian political actors and facilitated negotiations between conflicting parties. The organization's diplomatic efforts were instrumental in promoting reconciliation and fostering a peaceful political transition.

Moreover, the United Nations played a vital role in the humanitarian aspects of the intervention. It coordinated relief efforts and aid distribution, ensuring that the most vulnerable populations received the necessary assistance. This humanitarian support helped mitigate the impact of the intervention on Haitian society and economy, providing much-needed relief to a country ravaged by political instability and economic hardship.

The involvement of the United Nations in Operation Uphold Democracy had far-reaching diplomatic implications. It demonstrated the international community's commitment to upholding democratic principles and human rights. The intervention also underscored the importance of multilateral cooperation in addressing regional conflicts and promoting peace and security.

In conclusion, the United Nations' mandate and involvement in Operation Uphold Democracy were instrumental in achieving the objectives of the intervention. Through its diplomatic efforts, logistical support, and humanitarian assistance, the organization played a crucial role in restoring stability and democratic governance in Haiti. The intervention not only had immediate consequences for Haitian society and economy but also left a long-lasting legacy, shaping the country's political stability and democratic institutions for years to come.

The Role of UN Peacekeeping Forces in Haiti

The 1994 U.S.-led multinational military intervention in Haiti, also known as Operation Uphold Democracy, aimed to restore democracy and stability in the troubled nation. However, the success of this mission would not have been possible without the crucial role played by the United Nations (UN) peacekeeping forces. This subchapter will delve into the significance and impact of the UN peacekeeping forces in Haiti during and after Operation Uphold Democracy.

The UN peacekeeping forces played a pivotal role in maintaining security and order in Haiti throughout the intervention. Their primary objective was to create a safe environment for the return of exiled President Jean-Bertrand Aristide and to ensure the protection of civilians. The UN peacekeepers, under the mandate of the UN Security Council, were responsible for disarming and demobilizing the various armed factions that had plagued the country for years.

Additionally, the UN peacekeeping forces facilitated the restoration of the Haitian National Police (HNP) and assisted in the training and professionalization of its members. This was crucial in building a sustainable security apparatus capable of maintaining law and order in the long run. The UN also provided technical support and expertise to help rebuild Haiti's judicial system, further contributing to the establishment of a functioning democracy.

Furthermore, the UN peacekeeping forces played a vital role in the humanitarian aspects of the intervention. They coordinated relief efforts, distributed aid, and provided medical assistance to the Haitian population. Their presence helped alleviate the suffering of the people affected by the political instability and economic crisis that had plagued the country for decades.

The impact of the UN peacekeeping forces extended beyond the immediate intervention. Their continued presence in Haiti after Operation Uphold Democracy was crucial in ensuring the consolidation of democratic institutions and the prevention of a relapse into violence. The UN Stabilization Mission in Haiti (MINUSTAH) was established in 2004 to support the Haitian government in maintaining security, promoting human rights, and facilitating socioeconomic development.

In conclusion, the role of the UN peacekeeping forces in Haiti during and after Operation Uphold Democracy was instrumental in achieving the mission's objectives. Their efforts in maintaining security, supporting democratic institutions, and providing humanitarian assistance were crucial in restoring stability and bringing about positive change in Haiti. The long-term presence of the UN in Haiti through MINUSTAH further contributed to the consolidation of democracy and the prevention of further conflict. The success of Operation Uphold Democracy can, therefore, be attributed in large part to the significant role played by the UN peacekeeping forces.

The Coordination and Cooperation between the U.S. and the UN

One of the key aspects that shaped the outcome of Operation Uphold Democracy was the coordination and cooperation between the United States and the United Nations. This subchapter examines the intricate relationship between these two entities and the impact it had on the overall success or failure of the intervention.

From the outset, it became clear that the U.S. would take the lead in Operation Uphold Democracy, given its proximity to Haiti and its historical ties to the country. However, recognizing the need for international legitimacy and support, the U.S. sought the involvement of the United Nations. The UN played a crucial role in providing a multilateral framework for the intervention, which helped garner international support and legitimacy for the mission.

The coordination between the U.S. and the UN was exemplified by the establishment of the United Nations Mission in Haiti (UNMIH). This mission aimed to support the political process, restore public order, and promote human rights in Haiti. The U.S. and the UN worked together to develop a comprehensive strategy that encompassed both military and humanitarian aspects of the intervention.

While the U.S. provided the bulk of the military forces, the UN played a vital role in coordinating humanitarian efforts and aid distribution. The UN agencies, such as UNICEF and the World Food Programme, worked alongside U.S. military personnel to provide much-needed relief to the Haitian population. This cooperation ensured that humanitarian aid reached those who needed it the most, mitigating the impact of the crisis on Haitian society and economy.

Furthermore, the coordination between the U.S. and the UN extended to the political sphere. The UN facilitated the political transition in Haiti by overseeing the democratic elections and supporting the establishment of a stable government. This collaboration was crucial in ensuring the long-term stability and democratic development of Haiti.

However, the coordination and cooperation between the U.S. and the UN were not without challenges. There were instances where differing priorities and strategies led to tensions between the two entities. For example, while the U.S. focused on the military aspect of the intervention, the UN emphasized the importance of diplomatic and political solutions. These differences highlighted the complexities of multilateral operations and the need for effective coordination between various stakeholders.

In conclusion, the coordination and cooperation between the U.S. and the UN played a vital role in shaping the outcome of Operation Uphold Democracy. The involvement of the UN provided international legitimacy and support for the intervention, while also facilitating humanitarian efforts and political transition in Haiti. Despite some challenges, this collaboration between the U.S. and the UN contributed to the overall success of the mission and left a lasting impact on Haiti's political stability and democratic institutions.

The Challenges and Controversies Surrounding UN Involvement

The United Nations' involvement in Operation Uphold Democracy presented both challenges and controversies that had far-reaching implications for the success or failure of the mission. As historians delve into the intricacies of this U.S.-led multinational military intervention in Haiti, it becomes apparent that the UN played a pivotal role, but not without facing significant obstacles.

One of the main challenges encountered by the UN was the political history of Haiti before and after the U.S.-led intervention. Haiti had long been plagued by political instability, corruption, and human rights abuses. The UN had to navigate these complex dynamics to ensure a successful transition to democracy. However, deep-rooted political divisions and mistrust among various factions posed a significant challenge, making it difficult to build a consensus and establish a stable government.

Furthermore, the impact of Operation Uphold Democracy on Haitian society and economy created further controversy. The intervention aimed to restore democracy and improve living conditions for the Haitian people. However, the unintended consequences of the military intervention, such as collateral damage and disruptions to the economy, led to a backlash from segments of the Haitian population. Critics argued that the intervention failed to address the root causes of Haiti's problems and instead exacerbated them.

The international response and diplomatic implications of the intervention also generated heated debate. While the U.S. led the military operation, the involvement of other nations, particularly those in the region, sparked concerns about neo-colonialism and interference in Haiti's internal affairs. The UN's role in coordinating the multinational effort became a subject of scrutiny, as questions arose about the organization's impartiality and effectiveness in addressing the crisis.

Another controversial aspect was the media coverage and public perception of the intervention, both domestically and internationally. The media played a crucial role in shaping public opinion and influencing the narrative surrounding Operation Uphold Democracy. Some critics argued that the media's portrayal of the intervention was biased, focusing primarily on the military tactics employed rather than the humanitarian aspects and the long-term consequences for Haiti.

As historians analyze the legacy of Operation Uphold Democracy, they must consider the long-term consequences for Haiti's political stability and democratic institutions. While the intervention succeeded in restoring a semblance of democracy, its impact on the country's political landscape was not without challenges. The UN's involvement, though crucial, faced controversies that continue to shape perceptions of the operation's success or failure.

In conclusion, the challenges and controversies surrounding the UN's involvement in Operation Uphold Democracy cannot be overlooked. The political history of Haiti, the impact on society and the economy, the international response, military strategy, humanitarian aspects, and the long-term consequences all contribute to a multifaceted analysis of the intervention. Historians must carefully examine these factors to measure the success or failure of Operation Uphold Democracy in achieving its objectives and to understand its enduring legacy on Haiti's political stability and democratic institutions.

Chapter 4: The Impact of Operation Uphold Democracy on Haitian Society and Economy

The Humanitarian Crisis and the Effects on Haitian Society

The chapter titled "The Humanitarian Crisis and the Effects on Haitian Society" explores the impact of Operation Uphold Democracy on the people of Haiti and their social fabric. This subchapter delves into the humanitarian aspects of the intervention, including relief efforts and aid distribution, as well as the experiences and perspectives of Haitian civilians during and after the operation.

Operation Uphold Democracy, the 1994 U.S.-led multinational military intervention in Haiti, aimed to restore democracy and stability to the country. However, the intervention triggered a humanitarian crisis that had far-reaching consequences for Haitian society. The initial military operations disrupted essential services and infrastructure, exacerbating an already dire situation. The lack of access to clean water, food, and healthcare prompted a surge in disease outbreaks and malnutrition among the population.

Relief efforts were swiftly launched to address the humanitarian crisis. Humanitarian organizations and the U.S. military collaborated to provide aid and assistance to the affected population. However, the distribution of aid faced numerous challenges due to the destruction of infrastructure and logistical difficulties. Additionally, the influx of aid created a complex dynamic within Haitian society, with some communities receiving more support than others, leading to tensions and conflicts.

Haitian civilians experienced a wide range of emotions and perspectives during and after the operation. Some welcomed the intervention, believing it would bring stability and prosperity to their country. Others were skeptical, questioning the motives of the intervening forces and expressing concerns about the infringement of their sovereignty. Many Haitians endured hardships during the operation and its aftermath, grappling with the loss of loved ones, displacement, and a disrupted way of life.

The long-term consequences of Operation Uphold Democracy on Haiti's social fabric were profound. The intervention disrupted existing power structures and exacerbated existing divides within society. The combination of political instability, economic challenges, and social upheaval hindered the establishment of stable democratic institutions. The legacy of Operation Uphold Democracy continued to shape Haiti's political stability for years to come.

In conclusion, the humanitarian crisis caused by Operation Uphold Democracy had a profound impact on Haitian society. The relief efforts and aid distribution faced considerable challenges, and the experiences and perspectives of Haitian civilians varied widely. The long-term consequences of the intervention on Haiti's political stability and democratic institutions were significant, shaping the country's trajectory for years to come. Historians analyzing Operation Uphold Democracy must consider the complex humanitarian aspects and their effects on Haitian society as they evaluate the overall success or failure of the intervention.

Economic Consequences and Challenges Faced by Haiti

The economic consequences and challenges faced by Haiti following the U.S.-led intervention in 1994, known as Operation Uphold Democracy, were significant and had long-lasting effects on the country's economy. This subchapter explores the impact of the intervention on Haiti's economic stability and the challenges it faced in rebuilding and developing its economy.

Before the intervention, Haiti was already grappling with economic difficulties, including high levels of poverty, unemployment, and a weak infrastructure. The political instability further exacerbated these challenges, making it difficult for the country to attract foreign investment and promote economic growth.

Operation Uphold Democracy aimed to restore political stability in Haiti, but its economic impact was mixed. While the intervention initially brought about some short-term improvements, such as increased foreign aid and investment, it failed to address the underlying structural issues that hindered Haiti's economic development.

One of the major economic consequences of the intervention was the displacement of thousands of Haitian civilians, causing disruptions in agricultural production and exacerbating food insecurity. This, coupled with the destruction of infrastructure during the intervention, severely impacted the country's ability to recover and rebuild its economy.

Furthermore, the intervention did not effectively address corruption and mismanagement, which remained rampant in Haiti. This hindered efforts to attract foreign investment and create a favorable business environment, limiting economic growth and job creation.

The challenges faced by Haiti in the aftermath of the intervention were further compounded by the global economic downturn of the late 1990s and early 2000s. The country struggled to recover from the devastating impact of the intervention while also dealing with the effects of the global recession.

Despite these challenges, Haiti did experience some positive economic developments in the years following the intervention. The United Nations and other international organizations provided assistance and support for economic reconstruction and development projects.

Efforts were made to improve infrastructure, promote agriculture, and expand access to education and healthcare.

However, the long-term consequences of Operation Uphold Democracy on Haiti's economic stability and democratic institutions remain a subject of debate among historians. While some argue that the intervention helped stabilize the country and pave the way for economic reforms, others contend that it failed to address the root causes of Haiti's economic challenges and resulted in further dependency on foreign aid.

In conclusion, the economic consequences and challenges faced by Haiti following Operation Uphold Democracy were significant and continue to shape the country's economic trajectory. The intervention had mixed results in addressing Haiti's economic issues, and the long-term impact on the country's economic stability and democratic institutions remains a topic of discussion among historians.

The Reconstruction Efforts and their Long-term Implications

In the aftermath of Operation Uphold Democracy, the international community rallied to support Haiti in its path towards stability and democracy. This subchapter explores the reconstruction efforts that were undertaken and delves into their long-term implications for Haiti's political stability and democratic institutions.

The reconstruction efforts were multifaceted, addressing not only the physical infrastructure but also the social, economic, and political spheres of Haitian society. The United Nations played a crucial role in coordinating these efforts, working closely with the Haitian government and other international organizations to ensure a comprehensive approach.

One of the key areas of focus was the rebuilding of Haiti's political institutions. The U.S.-led intervention aimed to restore democratic governance, and significant efforts were made to strengthen Haiti's electoral system and support the development of political parties. The establishment of a stable and effective government was seen as essential for long-term political stability.

Economically, Operation Uphold Democracy aimed to jumpstart Haiti's struggling economy. The international community provided financial aid and technical assistance to promote economic growth and create employment opportunities. Investment in infrastructure projects, such as the rebuilding of roads and bridges, was also prioritized to facilitate trade and improve access to markets.

The reconstruction efforts had a profound impact on Haitian society. The provision of humanitarian aid, including food, water, and medical supplies, alleviated the immediate suffering caused by the political crisis and subsequent military intervention. However, the long-term implications were more complex. The influx of aid and international organizations had both positive and negative consequences. While it provided much-needed assistance, it also created a dependency on foreign aid and disrupted local markets.

Moreover, the experiences and perspectives of Haitian civilians during and after Operation Uphold Democracy varied greatly. While some welcomed the intervention as a means to restore stability and democracy, others felt that their voices and concerns were not adequately represented. The subchapter explores these differing perspectives and highlights the challenges faced by Haitian civilians in the aftermath of the intervention.

Ultimately, the assessment of the success or failure of Operation Uphold Democracy in achieving its objectives is a topic of debate among historians. Some argue that it succeeded in restoring political stability and democracy, while others highlight the ongoing challenges faced by Haiti in these areas.

The subchapter concludes by examining the long-term consequences and legacy of Operation Uphold Democracy on Haiti's political stability and democratic institutions. It considers whether the intervention had a lasting impact or if the gains made were temporary. It also explores the wider diplomatic implications and the media coverage and public perception of the intervention, both domestically and internationally.

Overall, the reconstruction efforts following Operation Uphold Democracy had a significant impact on Haiti's political, economic, and social landscape. Understanding these efforts and their long-term implications is crucial for historians seeking to measure the success or failure of the intervention and its impact on Haiti's democratic development.

The Social and Cultural Transformations in Post-Intervention Haiti

In the aftermath of Operation Uphold Democracy, Haiti experienced significant social and cultural transformations that continue to shape the nation to this day. This subchapter explores the various changes that occurred in the wake of the 1994 U.S.-led multinational military intervention, shedding light on the long-term consequences and legacy of the operation.

One of the most notable social transformations was the impact on Haitian society and economy. Operation Uphold Democracy aimed to restore political stability and democratic institutions in Haiti, and while progress was made in these areas, the intervention also brought about unintended consequences. The influx of international aid and the presence of foreign troops led to changes in the local economy, with some sectors benefiting from the increased demand, while others suffered from increased competition. Additionally, the intervention disrupted social structures and created tensions within Haitian society, as different factions vied for power and influence.

Furthermore, the experiences and perspectives of Haitian civilians during and after Operation Uphold Democracy provide valuable insights into the social and cultural changes that took place. Many Haitians welcomed the intervention as a means to end the political turmoil and violence that had plagued the nation for years. However, there were also instances of human rights abuses and violence committed by both sides during the intervention, which left a lasting impact on the collective memory of the Haitian people.

The international response and diplomatic implications of the intervention played a crucial role in shaping post-intervention Haiti. The United Nations played a significant role in supporting the intervention and assisting with the transition to democracy. However, there were also tensions between Haiti and the international community, particularly regarding issues of sovereignty and national pride.

The media coverage and public perception of the intervention, both domestically and internationally, also played a part in shaping post-intervention Haiti. The media played a significant role in shaping public opinion and influencing the narrative surrounding the intervention. The portrayal of Haiti in the media had a lasting impact on how the country was perceived and treated by the international community.

In conclusion, the social and cultural transformations in post-intervention Haiti were complex and multifaceted. Operation Uphold Democracy had both positive and negative impacts on Haitian society and economy. The experiences of Haitian civilians, the international response, and the media coverage all played a role in shaping the legacy of the intervention. Understanding these transformations is crucial for historians seeking to assess the success or failure of Operation Uphold Democracy and its long-term consequences on Haiti's political stability and democratic institutions.

Assessing the Overall Impact on Haitian Society and Economy

Operation Uphold Democracy: Measuring Success or Failure in Objectives Achieved

Haiti, a nation plagued by political instability and economic struggles, witnessed a significant turning point in its history with Operation Uphold Democracy, the 1994 U.S.-led multinational military intervention. This subchapter aims to evaluate the overall impact of this intervention on Haitian society and economy, shedding light on the long-term consequences and legacy it left behind.

Operation Uphold Democracy had a profound effect on Haiti's society, challenging its political history before and after the intervention. Prior to the U.S.-led intervention, Haiti had experienced a series of military coups, undermining democratic institutions. The operation sought to restore stability, strengthen democratic governance, and promote respect for human rights. While it achieved some success in stabilizing the political landscape, the long-term impact remains debatable.

Economically, Haiti faced numerous challenges even before Operation Uphold Democracy. The intervention aimed to revitalize the economy, attract foreign investment, and foster sustainable development. However, the desired economic transformation did not materialize as expected. The intervention's short-term relief efforts and aid distribution were commendable, but they failed to address the underlying socioeconomic issues plaguing the nation.

The United Nations played a crucial role in Operation Uphold Democracy, collaborating with the United States and other participating nations. Their involvement focused on providing peacekeeping forces, assisting with political transition, and supporting humanitarian efforts. The UN's presence helped maintain stability and contributed to the overall success of the intervention.

Assessing the success or failure of Operation Uphold Democracy requires a comprehensive examination of its military strategy and tactics. The intervention's military approach effectively restored security, disarmed paramilitary groups, and facilitated the return of exiled President Jean-Bertrand Aristide. However, questions arise regarding the proportionality of force used and the potential impact on civilian casualties.

The experiences and perspectives of Haitian civilians during and after Operation Uphold Democracy provide valuable insights. While some civilians welcomed the intervention as a means to end violence and oppression, others felt disillusioned as their expectations for a better future were not fully realized. Their voices are crucial in evaluating the intervention's impact.

Furthermore, the international response and diplomatic implications of Operation Uphold Democracy cannot be overlooked. The intervention received mixed reactions globally, with some countries supporting the mission while others questioned its motives. Analyzing the media coverage and public perception domestically and internationally can provide a comprehensive understanding of how the intervention was perceived.

Lastly, the long-term consequences and legacy of Operation Uphold Democracy on Haiti's political stability and democratic institutions must be examined. Did the intervention succeed in establishing a lasting democratic framework, or did it merely serve as a temporary solution? Evaluating the intervention's impact on political stability and democratic institutions will shed light on its effectiveness in achieving its objectives.

In conclusion, assessing the overall impact of Operation Uphold Democracy on Haitian society and economy requires a multidimensional analysis. Understanding its effects on historical, political, economic, and social aspects is crucial in determining the success or failure of the intervention. By examining the experiences of Haitian civilians, the role of the United Nations, the military strategy employed, and the long-term consequences, historians can paint a comprehensive picture of this significant chapter in Haiti's history.

Chapter 5: The International Response and Diplomatic Implications of the Intervention

The Reactions and Responses from Regional and Global Actors

One of the key aspects to analyze when assessing the success or failure of Operation Uphold Democracy is the reactions and responses from regional and global actors. The intervention, led by the United States in 1994, aimed to restore political stability and democracy in Haiti. This subchapter will delve into the various actors involved and their contributions to the operation.

Regionally, the response to Operation Uphold Democracy was mixed. The Caribbean Community (CARICOM) countries, including Jamaica and Trinidad and Tobago, expressed support for the intervention. These nations recognized the importance of restoring democracy in Haiti and the potential for instability to spill over into neighboring countries. They provided diplomatic and logistical assistance to the multinational force, underscoring the regional commitment to resolving the crisis.

On the other hand, some regional actors, such as Cuba and Venezuela, criticized the United States' intervention as an infringement on Haiti's sovereignty. These countries viewed the operation as another example of U.S. imperialism in the region and condemned the military approach to resolving the political crisis. Their opposition to Operation Uphold Democracy led to strained diplomatic relations with the United States, complicating the intervention's broader implications.

At the global level, the response to Operation Uphold Democracy was similarly varied. The United Nations played a crucial role in the intervention, providing legitimacy and coordination. The UN Security Council passed resolutions authorizing the use of force and establishing the United Nations Mission in Haiti (UNMIH) to oversee the transition to democracy. The involvement of the UN demonstrated the international community's commitment to supporting democratic processes and upholding human rights.

However, some global actors expressed skepticism about the U.S.-led intervention. European countries, for instance, questioned the legality and effectiveness of military intervention in resolving political crises. They emphasized the need for diplomatic solutions and expressed concerns about potential civilian casualties and human rights abuses during the operation. These divergent views highlighted the complexities of international relations and the challenges of achieving consensus on interventionist policies.

Overall, the reactions and responses from regional and global actors to Operation Uphold Democracy reflected a combination of support, opposition, and skepticism. The intervention brought together a multinational coalition with diverse perspectives on how best to restore democracy in Haiti. Understanding these reactions and responses is crucial to comprehending the broader diplomatic implications of the intervention and its long-term consequences on Haiti's political stability and democratic institutions.

The Diplomatic Efforts to Support or Oppose the Intervention

The success or failure of any military intervention often hinges on the diplomatic efforts made to gather support or opposition from various nations. Operation Uphold Democracy, the 1994 U.S.-led multinational military intervention in Haiti, was no exception. This subchapter delves into the diplomatic strategies employed by the United States and other stakeholders in garnering international support or opposition for the intervention.

The United States, as the leading force behind Operation Uphold Democracy, faced the task of rallying international support for its mission in Haiti. Diplomatic efforts were made to secure backing from key nations, such as France and Canada, as well as regional organizations like the Organization of American States (OAS). These efforts involved presenting a compelling case for intervention, emphasizing the importance of restoring democracy and stability in Haiti, and addressing concerns raised by potential opponents.

On the other hand, there were also diplomatic efforts made by countries and organizations opposed to the intervention. Some nations, including China and Russia, expressed reservations about the U.S.-led intervention, citing concerns over the violation of sovereignty and the potential for a precedent-setting intervention. These opposing voices sought to rally support against the intervention by highlighting these concerns and urging diplomatic solutions instead.

The United Nations also played a significant role in Operation Uphold Democracy. Diplomatic efforts were made to secure a UN Security Council resolution authorizing the intervention, which required delicate negotiations and compromises. The involvement of the United Nations lent legitimacy to the intervention and provided a platform for diplomatic discussions among member states.

The diplomatic implications of the intervention extended beyond the immediate support or opposition for the mission. They influenced the perception of the intervention both domestically and internationally, shaping public opinion and media coverage. The success of the diplomatic efforts in garnering support or opposition also had long-term consequences on Haiti's political stability and democratic institutions.

Understanding the diplomatic efforts surrounding Operation Uphold Democracy provides historians with valuable insights into the complexities of international relations and the role of diplomacy in military interventions. By examining the strategies employed by various nations and organizations, historians can assess the effectiveness of these efforts and their impact on the intervention's outcome.

In conclusion, the diplomatic efforts to support or oppose the intervention in Operation Uphold Democracy were crucial in shaping the international response to the mission. The United States, supported by key nations and organizations, sought to gather international backing for the intervention, while opponents raised concerns over sovereignty and legality. The diplomatic implications of the intervention extended beyond the immediate mission, impacting public perception, media coverage, and Haiti's long-term political stability. Analyzing these diplomatic efforts provides historians with a comprehensive understanding of the complexities surrounding military interventions and their wider implications.

The Role of International Organizations in Shaping the Intervention's Outcome

One of the key factors that influenced the outcome of Operation Uphold Democracy, the 1994 U.S.-led multinational military intervention in Haiti, was the involvement of international organizations. These organizations played a crucial role in shaping the overall outcome of the intervention, both in terms of its immediate objectives and its long-term consequences on Haiti's political stability and democratic institutions.

The United Nations (UN) played a central role in Operation Uphold Democracy, providing the legal framework and support necessary for the intervention to take place. The UN Security Council passed Resolution 940, which authorized the use of force to restore democracy in Haiti and established the UN Mission in Haiti (UNMIH) to oversee the intervention. The UNMIH coordinated the efforts of the multinational forces and worked closely with Haitian authorities to ensure a smooth transition to democracy.

In addition to the UN, other international organizations such as the Organization of American States (OAS) and the Caribbean Community (CARICOM) also played important roles in shaping the intervention's outcome. The OAS provided diplomatic support and helped facilitate negotiations between the Haitian government and the international community. CARICOM, comprised of Caribbean nations, played a crucial role in ensuring regional stability and support for the intervention.

The involvement of these international organizations not only helped legitimize the intervention but also provided a framework for the delivery of humanitarian aid and the restoration of essential services in Haiti. These organizations played a key role in coordinating relief efforts, aid distribution, and the rebuilding of Haiti's economy and infrastructure.

However, the role of international organizations in shaping the intervention's outcome was not without challenges. The complex political dynamics in Haiti, coupled with the socio-economic challenges facing the country, posed significant obstacles to the successful implementation of the intervention's objectives. The ability of these organizations to navigate these challenges and effectively engage with the Haitian government and society had a direct impact on the intervention's overall success.

In conclusion, the involvement of international organizations was instrumental in shaping the outcome of Operation Uphold Democracy. Their coordination efforts, diplomatic support, and provision of humanitarian aid were crucial in achieving the objectives of the intervention. However, the challenges faced in implementing these objectives highlight the complex nature of interventions and the need for careful coordination and engagement with the host country. The role of international organizations in shaping the intervention's outcome provides valuable insights for historians studying the impact of Operation Uphold Democracy on Haiti's political history, society, and economy.

The Long-term Diplomatic Implications for Haiti and its Relations with the International Community

When examining the long-term diplomatic implications for Haiti following the U.S.-led intervention in 1994, it is crucial to consider the political history of the country both before and after Operation Uphold Democracy. Haiti has a tumultuous past characterized by political instability and economic challenges. The intervention sought to restore democratic governance and stability to the nation, but its impact on Haiti's relations with the international community cannot be overlooked.

Operation Uphold Democracy, led by the United States, was a multinational military intervention aimed at removing the military junta that had seized power in Haiti. The United Nations played a crucial role in supporting the intervention and facilitating the transition to democratic rule. This cooperation and support from the international community highlighted the importance of Haiti's stability to the global stage.

In terms of the impact on Haitian society and economy, Operation Uphold Democracy brought about significant changes. The intervention led to the return of the democratically elected President Jean-Bertrand Aristide and the restoration of democratic institutions. However, challenges remained in rebuilding the economy and addressing social issues. The international community's involvement in relief efforts and aid distribution was a crucial aspect of the intervention's humanitarian aspects.

The experiences and perspectives of Haitian civilians during and after Operation Uphold Democracy vary. While some welcomed the intervention as a means to restore democracy and stability, others criticized the international involvement and its potential to undermine Haiti's sovereignty. Understanding the diverse perspectives of the Haitian people is essential in assessing the overall success or failure of the intervention.

Media coverage and public perception of the intervention, both domestically and internationally, played a crucial role in shaping its legacy. The intervention received mixed reviews, with some praising it as a successful operation and others questioning its long-term effectiveness. This media coverage and public perception influenced Haiti's relationship with the international community and its standing in the global arena.

The long-term consequences and legacy of Operation Uphold Democracy on Haiti's political stability and democratic institutions are still evident today. While the intervention succeeded in restoring democracy in the short term, Haiti continues to face challenges in achieving lasting political stability. The impact of the intervention on Haiti's diplomatic relations with the international community remains a topic of ongoing debate among historians and scholars.

In conclusion, the long-term diplomatic implications of Operation Uphold Democracy for Haiti and its relations with the international community are complex and multifaceted. The intervention had both positive and negative consequences, and its legacy continues to shape Haiti's political stability and democratic institutions. Understanding these implications is crucial for historians and those interested in the history of Operation Uphold Democracy.

Chapter 6: The Military Strategy and Tactics Employed during Operation Uphold Democracy

The Planning and Execution of the Military Operation

The planning and execution of a military operation is a critical aspect that determines its success or failure. Operation Uphold Democracy, the 1994 U.S.-led multinational military intervention in Haiti, was no exception. This subchapter delves into the intricacies of the planning and execution of this operation, shedding light on the key factors that influenced its outcome.

The planning phase of Operation Uphold Democracy involved meticulous analysis of the political history of Haiti before and after the intervention. Historians studying this operation will find valuable insights into the complex dynamics that shaped Haiti's political landscape and influenced the decision-making process behind the intervention. Understanding the role of the United Nations in this operation is also crucial, as it highlights the collaborative efforts and diplomatic implications that accompanied the military intervention.

The military strategy and tactics employed during Operation Uphold Democracy were instrumental in achieving its objectives. Historians interested in military history will find a comprehensive examination of the strategies employed by the multinational forces, including the utilization of air power, ground operations, and intelligence gathering. The subchapter also explores the humanitarian aspects of the intervention, including relief efforts and aid distribution, providing a holistic understanding of the operation's impact on Haitian society and economy.

To fully comprehend the consequences of Operation Uphold Democracy, it is essential to analyze the experiences and perspectives of Haitian civilians during and after the intervention. This subchapter offers a platform for historians to explore the voices of those directly affected by the operation, shedding light on their hopes, fears, and aspirations.

Furthermore, the assessment of the success or failure of Operation Uphold Democracy in achieving its objectives is a critical aspect for historians. By examining the media coverage and public perception of the intervention, both domestically and internationally, this subchapter provides a comprehensive analysis of how the operation was perceived and understood by different stakeholders.

Finally, the long-term consequences and legacy of Operation Uphold Democracy on Haiti's political stability and democratic institutions are explored. Historians will find a detailed examination of how the intervention shaped Haiti's future, including its impact on political stability, democratic governance, and the country's overall trajectory.

In conclusion, this subchapter offers historians a comprehensive analysis of the planning and execution of Operation Uphold Democracy. By delving into the military strategy, humanitarian aspects, and long-term consequences, this content provides a valuable resource for understanding the complexities of this significant military intervention in Haiti.

The Role of Air and Naval Forces in the Intervention

In the subchapter titled "The Role of Air and Naval Forces in the Intervention," we delve into the critical role played by air and naval forces during Operation Uphold Democracy. This chapter aims to provide historians with a comprehensive understanding of the strategic importance of these forces in achieving the objectives of the intervention in Haiti.

During Operation Uphold Democracy, the deployment of air and naval forces proved instrumental in several ways. Firstly, the air superiority provided by the United States Air Force played a crucial role in neutralizing the Haitian military's capabilities. Through precision airstrikes, the air forces targeted strategic military installations and key infrastructure, severely hampering the oppressive regime's ability to maintain control.

Naval forces also played a pivotal role in the operation. The U.S. Navy, in collaboration with other international naval forces, established a formidable blockade around Haiti, effectively preventing the flow of weapons and supplies to the illegitimate regime. This blockade not only limited the regime's ability to further oppress the Haitian people but also demonstrated the international community's commitment to the restoration of democracy.

Furthermore, the naval forces facilitated the transport of troops and equipment, ensuring swift deployment of ground forces. The ability to quickly move troops and supplies by sea expedited the intervention, allowing for a rapid response to the evolving situation on the ground.

The subchapter also explores the coordination between air and naval forces, highlighting the synergy achieved through joint operations. The close collaboration between the air force and navy facilitated effective communication, intelligence sharing, and coordinated strikes, maximizing the impact on the regime while minimizing the risk to both military personnel and civilians.

Additionally, the chapter examines the humanitarian aspect of the intervention, focusing on the role of air and naval forces in relief efforts and aid distribution. The air force and navy played a crucial role in providing logistical support for delivering humanitarian aid to the affected population, ensuring the well-being of the Haitian people amidst the chaos of the intervention.

Overall, the subchapter on the role of air and naval forces in the intervention sheds light on the pivotal contribution of these forces in achieving the objectives of Operation Uphold Democracy. By analyzing their strategic importance and operational effectiveness, historians can gain a profound understanding of the military dimension of the intervention and its impact on Haiti's political stability and democratic institutions.

The Ground Operations and Counterinsurgency Efforts

During Operation Uphold Democracy, the United States-led multinational military intervention in Haiti in 1994, ground operations and counterinsurgency efforts played a crucial role in achieving the mission's objectives. This subchapter examines the strategies and tactics employed to restore stability and democracy in Haiti.

Following President Jean-Bertrand Aristide's forced exile, Haiti plunged into a state of political turmoil. Armed groups and paramilitary organizations emerged, posing a significant threat to the restoration of democratic governance. The multinational force, under the command of the United States, devised a comprehensive military strategy to counter these insurgents and create a secure environment for the Haitian people.

Counterinsurgency efforts focused on disrupting the command and control structures of armed groups while minimizing civilian casualties. A combination of intelligence-driven operations, targeted raids, and coordinated air and ground campaigns was employed to dismantle these organizations. The multinational force worked closely with Haitian security forces to enhance their capacity and ensure a smooth transition of power once stability was restored.

Ground operations were conducted in close collaboration with the United Nations, which provided vital support in terms of logistics, intelligence, and peacekeeping forces. The multinational force worked within the framework of UN Security Council resolutions to ensure international legitimacy and diplomatic support.

In addition to military operations, the intervention also had a significant humanitarian aspect. Relief efforts and aid distribution played a crucial role in winning the hearts and minds of the Haitian people. The multinational force worked tirelessly to provide essential services, such as healthcare, food, and clean water, to communities affected by the conflict. These efforts not only alleviated immediate suffering but also helped build trust and support for the intervention.

The experiences and perspectives of Haitian civilians during and after Operation Uphold Democracy were diverse. While some welcomed the intervention as a necessary step towards restoring democracy, others expressed concerns about the long-term consequences and the potential erosion of Haitian sovereignty. It is essential to consider these viewpoints when assessing the success or failure of the operation in achieving its objectives.

The media coverage and public perception of the intervention, both domestically and internationally, also played a significant role in shaping public opinion. While some media outlets praised the multinational force for its efforts, others criticized the intervention as an infringement on Haiti's sovereignty. Understanding these narratives is crucial to comprehensively evaluate the impact and legacy of Operation Uphold Democracy.

In conclusion, the ground operations and counterinsurgency efforts were instrumental in achieving the objectives of Operation Uphold Democracy. The multinational force, working in collaboration with the United Nations, employed a comprehensive military strategy, combined with humanitarian aid, to restore stability and democracy in Haiti. However, the assessment of success or failure must consider the experiences and perspectives of Haitian civilians, media coverage, and the long-term consequences on Haiti's political stability and democratic institutions.

The Lessons Learned and Critiques of the Military Strategy

In the subchapter titled "The Lessons Learned and Critiques of the Military Strategy," we delve into the military tactics employed during Operation Uphold Democracy and critically evaluate their effectiveness in achieving the mission's objectives. This analysis is crucial for historians, as it provides valuable insights into the intricacies of this U.S.-led multinational military intervention in Haiti in 1994.

Operation Uphold Democracy was a complex mission that aimed to restore stability and democracy to Haiti after a tumultuous period of political instability. The military strategy employed during the operation involved a combination of air power, ground forces, and naval support. The primary objective was to remove the military dictatorship of General Raoul Cédras and reinstate President Jean-Bertrand Aristide, who had been democratically elected.

One of the key lessons learned from Operation Uphold Democracy was the importance of a comprehensive and integrated approach. While the military intervention was successful in achieving its immediate objective of removing the dictatorship, the long-term stability and democratic institution-building in Haiti were not adequately addressed. The lack of a holistic strategy led to challenges in maintaining security and establishing effective governance structures in the post-intervention period.

Critiques of the military strategy employed during Operation Uphold Democracy also focus on the potential overreliance on force. While military force was necessary to remove the dictatorship, some argue that a more nuanced and diplomatic approach could have been pursued to ensure a smoother transition and minimize the impact on the civilian population. The use of force, particularly in densely populated areas, resulted in collateral damage and raised concerns about the humanitarian aspects of the intervention.

Furthermore, the evaluation of the military strategy highlights the importance of coordination and collaboration between the U.S. and international partners, particularly the United Nations. The involvement of the United Nations provided legitimacy to the intervention and enabled a more inclusive and multilateral approach. However, challenges in coordination and communication between the various actors were evident, and these issues impacted the effectiveness of the military strategy.

Overall, the analysis of the military strategy employed during Operation Uphold Democracy offers valuable lessons for future military interventions. It emphasizes the need for a comprehensive and integrated approach that considers the long-term stability and democratic institution-building. Additionally, it underscores the significance of coordination and collaboration between international partners to ensure the success of such interventions.

The subchapter also delves into the critiques of the military strategy, highlighting the potential overreliance on force and the need for a more nuanced and diplomatic approach. By critically evaluating the military tactics used, historians can gain a deeper understanding of the complexities and challenges associated with Operation Uphold Democracy, providing valuable insights for future interventions.

Chapter 7: The Humanitarian Aspects of the Intervention, including Relief Efforts and Aid Distribution

The Humanitarian Crisis and the Need for Assistance

In the chapter titled "The Humanitarian Crisis and the Need for Assistance," we delve into the dire circumstances that unfolded during Operation Uphold Democracy, the 1994 U.S.-led multinational military intervention in Haiti. This chapter aims to provide historians with an in-depth understanding of the humanitarian aspects of the intervention, including relief efforts and aid distribution.

The political history of Haiti before and after the U.S.-led intervention sets the stage for the magnitude of the crisis that unfolded. Decades of political instability, economic struggles, and social unrest had left the Haitian society vulnerable and on the brink of collapse. Operation Uphold Democracy aimed to restore stability, democracy, and provide much-needed humanitarian assistance to the Haitian people.

The United Nations played a crucial role in Operation Uphold Democracy, working alongside the United States and other participating nations to provide assistance and coordinate relief efforts. Their involvement ensured a unified and coordinated approach to addressing the humanitarian crisis.

Relief efforts during Operation Uphold Democracy were extensive and varied. Humanitarian aid, including food, medicine, and shelter, was provided to the affected population. The distribution of aid posed significant challenges, with limited resources and infrastructure. However, the international community's commitment to assisting Haiti helped alleviate some of the immediate suffering faced by the Haitian people.

The experiences and perspectives of Haitian civilians during and after Operation Uphold Democracy offer valuable insights into the impact of the intervention on their lives. Their narratives provide a human element to the crisis, shedding light on the struggles they faced and the long-lasting effects on their communities.

Assessing the success or failure of Operation Uphold Democracy in achieving its objectives is a critical aspect of understanding its impact. Historians can analyze the effectiveness of the relief efforts, the degree of stability restored, and the long-term consequences on Haiti's political stability and democratic institutions.

Furthermore, the media coverage and public perception of the intervention, both domestically and internationally, shaped the narrative surrounding Operation Uphold Democracy. Understanding how the intervention was portrayed and perceived can provide historians with insights into the broader diplomatic implications and international response.

The chapter concludes with an exploration of the long-term consequences and legacy of Operation Uphold Democracy on Haiti's political stability and democratic institutions. By examining the post-intervention period, historians can evaluate the lasting impact of the intervention and its implications for Haiti's future.

In summary, "The Humanitarian Crisis and the Need for Assistance" chapter offers historians a comprehensive analysis of the relief efforts and aid distribution during Operation Uphold Democracy. By examining the experiences of Haitian civilians, assessing the intervention's success, and exploring its long-term consequences, this chapter sheds light on the humanitarian aspects of the intervention.

The Relief Efforts and Aid Distribution Mechanisms

One of the crucial aspects of Operation Uphold Democracy was the humanitarian response and aid distribution mechanisms put in place to alleviate the suffering of the Haitian population. In the wake of the U.S.-led intervention, Haiti faced a dire humanitarian crisis, characterized by widespread poverty, a crumbling infrastructure, and a lack of basic necessities. The relief efforts aimed to address these challenges and improve the overall well-being of the Haitian people.

The United Nations played a significant role in coordinating the relief efforts and ensuring the effective distribution of aid. Working in collaboration with various international organizations and NGOs, the UN established a comprehensive relief network that encompassed food distribution, healthcare services, and infrastructure rehabilitation. This coordinated approach ensured that aid reached those in need in a timely and efficient manner.

Food distribution formed a vital component of the relief efforts. The United Nations World Food Programme (WFP) played a crucial role in providing emergency food assistance to the Haitian population. Through a network of distribution centers, the WFP ensured that essential food items reached the most vulnerable sections of society, including children, the elderly, and those affected by displacement.

In addition to food aid, healthcare services were also prioritized. The United Nations Children's Fund (UNICEF) and other organizations focused on providing medical assistance, immunizations, and access to clean water and sanitation facilities. These efforts aimed to combat the rampant diseases and health challenges prevalent in post-intervention Haiti.

Efforts were also made to rehabilitate the country's infrastructure and restore essential services. The United Nations Development Programme (UNDP) played a key role in this regard, working to rebuild schools, hospitals, and other critical public facilities. This not only improved the quality of life for Haitians but also laid the foundation for long-term stability and development.

While the relief efforts and aid distribution mechanisms were vital in addressing the immediate needs of the Haitian population, challenges remained. The sheer scale of the crisis, coupled with the lack of resources and infrastructure, posed significant hurdles to effective aid delivery. Moreover, the humanitarian response was not without criticism, with some arguing that the efforts did not adequately address the underlying socio-economic issues that contributed to the crisis.

Nevertheless, the relief efforts and aid distribution mechanisms implemented during Operation Uphold Democracy played a crucial role in alleviating the suffering of the Haitian population. They provided much-needed assistance and laid the groundwork for long-term recovery and development. The experiences and perspectives of Haitian civilians during and after the intervention shed light on the impact of these relief efforts, ultimately contributing to the assessment of the success or failure of Operation Uphold Democracy in achieving its objectives.

The Challenges and Successes in Delivering Humanitarian Aid

Humanitarian aid is a critical aspect of any military intervention, and Operation Uphold Democracy in Haiti was no exception. This subchapter will explore the challenges and successes encountered in delivering humanitarian aid during the operation.

One of the major challenges faced by the multinational forces was the sheer magnitude of the humanitarian crisis in Haiti. The country was already grappling with widespread poverty, political instability, and a crumbling infrastructure. The arrival of the multinational forces only exacerbated these issues, as large numbers of displaced people and a surge in violence created an urgent need for assistance.

Another challenge was the logistical nightmare of delivering aid to the affected regions. Haiti's mountainous terrain, poor road networks, and limited resources made it extremely difficult to transport food, water, and medical supplies to the areas most in need. Additionally, the presence of armed gangs and the risk of violent attacks posed significant security concerns for aid workers.

Despite these challenges, there were notable successes in delivering humanitarian aid during Operation Uphold Democracy. The United Nations played a crucial role in coordinating relief efforts and ensuring that aid reached its intended recipients. The UN's presence also helped establish a sense of stability and security, which was essential for aid distribution.

The international response to the crisis was also commendable. Several countries, including the United States, Canada, and France, provided significant financial and material aid to support relief efforts. Non-governmental organizations and humanitarian agencies also played a pivotal role in delivering aid and providing essential services to the affected population.

However, it is important to acknowledge that there were shortcomings and criticisms regarding the delivery of humanitarian aid. Some argued that aid distribution was not always efficient or equitable, and that certain regions or communities were neglected. Others contended that the relief efforts focused too heavily on short-term solutions, without addressing the underlying structural issues that perpetuated poverty and instability in Haiti.

To fully understand the challenges and successes in delivering humanitarian aid, it is essential to examine the experiences and perspectives of Haitian civilians. Their voices offer valuable insights into the effectiveness of relief efforts and the impact on their lives and communities.

In conclusion, delivering humanitarian aid during Operation Uphold Democracy presented numerous challenges, including the scale of the crisis, logistical difficulties, and security concerns. However, through international coordination, the involvement of the United Nations, and the support of various countries and organizations, significant progress was made in providing relief to the affected population. Nevertheless, there were areas for improvement, and it is crucial to consider the perspectives of Haitian civilians to ensure that future interventions prioritize their needs and address the root causes of Haiti's ongoing challenges.

The Role of NGOs and International Organizations in the Humanitarian Response

In the aftermath of the 1994 U.S.-led multinational military intervention in Haiti, known as Operation Uphold Democracy, the role of non-governmental organizations (NGOs) and international organizations in the humanitarian response was crucial. Historians studying this period have recognized the significant impact of NGOs and international organizations in providing relief efforts and aid distribution, as well as their long-term consequences on Haiti's political stability and democratic institutions.

NGOs played a vital role in delivering humanitarian assistance to the Haitian people during and after Operation Uphold Democracy. Organizations such as Médecins Sans Frontières (Doctors Without Borders) and Oxfam International were at the forefront of providing medical care, clean water, and food supplies to those affected by the intervention. These NGOs were able to mobilize quickly and efficiently, utilizing their expertise in humanitarian aid to address the immediate needs of the Haitian population. Their presence was particularly significant in areas where the government's capacity to respond was limited.

International organizations, such as the United Nations (UN), also played a crucial role in the humanitarian response. The UN established the United Nations Mission in Haiti (UNMIH) to oversee the transition to a stable and democratically elected government. Additionally, the UN coordinated efforts with NGOs to ensure the efficient distribution of aid and to address the long-term consequences of the intervention. The UNMIH's presence provided a sense of security and stability, which was essential for the success of relief efforts and the rebuilding process.

The collaboration between NGOs and international organizations was instrumental in addressing the complex challenges faced by Haitian society and economy. Together, they worked to rebuild infrastructure, improve healthcare systems, and promote sustainable development. Their efforts aimed to establish a foundation for long-term stability and democratic governance in Haiti, ensuring that the intervention's objectives were not limited to military success alone.

However, the effectiveness and impact of NGOs and international organizations in the humanitarian response should also be critically examined. Historians should explore the extent to which aid was distributed equitably and reached those most in need. They should also assess the long-term consequences of these interventions on Haiti's political stability and democratic institutions. By evaluating these aspects, historians can provide a comprehensive analysis of the role played by NGOs and international organizations in Operation Uphold Democracy and its aftermath.

Overall, the involvement of NGOs and international organizations in the humanitarian response following Operation Uphold Democracy was pivotal. Their presence not only addressed the immediate needs of the Haitian population but also played a vital role in the long-term stability and development of the country. By studying their role, historians can gain valuable insights into the successes and failures of the intervention and its impact on Haiti's political history and democratic institutions.

Chapter 8: The Experiences and Perspectives of Haitian Civilians during and after Operation Uphold Democracy

The Voices of Haitian Civilians during the Intervention

The subchapter titled "The Voices of Haitian Civilians during the Intervention" explores the experiences and perspectives of the Haitian population during and after Operation Uphold Democracy. This chapter aims to shed light on the impact of the intervention on ordinary Haitian civilians and provide a comprehensive understanding of their voices in this tumultuous period of the country's history.

Through extensive interviews and first-hand accounts from Haitian civilians, this subchapter unveils the diverse range of experiences and opinions during Operation Uphold Democracy. It delves into the lives of individuals affected by the intervention, including those who witnessed violence and upheaval, as well as those who experienced relief efforts and aid distribution.

These personal narratives offer valuable insights into the complexities of the intervention and its effects on Haitian society and economy. From the perspective of historians, these accounts provide a nuanced understanding of the intervention's impact on various aspects of Haitian life, such as political stability, democratic institutions, and even the everyday lives of the people.

Moreover, this subchapter explores the challenges faced by Haitian civilians in the aftermath of the intervention. It examines the long-term consequences and legacy of Operation Uphold Democracy on Haiti's political stability and democratic institutions. By examining the perspectives of Haitian civilians, historians can gain a more comprehensive understanding of the intervention's success or failure in achieving its objectives.

This subchapter also addresses the media coverage and public perception of the intervention, both domestically and internationally. By analyzing how the voices of Haitian civilians were represented in the media, historians can evaluate the accuracy and bias in the portrayal of the intervention.

Overall, the subchapter "The Voices of Haitian Civilians during the Intervention" provides historians with a unique and invaluable perspective on Operation Uphold Democracy. By incorporating the experiences and perspectives of Haitian civilians, this subchapter enriches the historical analysis of the intervention and contributes to a more comprehensive understanding of its impact on Haiti's political history, society, and economy.

The Impact on Human Rights and Civil Liberties in Haiti

The chapter titled "The Impact on Human Rights and Civil Liberties in Haiti" delves into the multifaceted consequences of Operation Uphold Democracy on the human rights and civil liberties of the Haitian population. This subchapter examines the extent to which the U.S.-led intervention succeeded or failed in upholding these fundamental principles.

Operation Uphold Democracy, initiated in 1994, aimed to restore democracy and stability in Haiti following years of political turmoil and human rights abuses. However, the intervention itself had unintended consequences on the very rights it sought to protect. While it successfully ousted the military regime and reinstated President Jean-Bertrand Aristide, the methods employed during the operation resulted in significant human rights violations.

The use of force by the multinational military coalition, including aerial bombardments and ground operations, led to civilian casualties and widespread displacement. These actions raised concerns about the excessive use of force and the failure to prioritize the protection of civilian lives. Human rights organizations documented numerous cases of extrajudicial killings, torture, and arbitrary arrests committed by both the military forces and local police.

Furthermore, the intervention inadvertently exacerbated existing social and economic inequalities in Haiti. The disruption caused by the military intervention hindered the already fragile infrastructure, exacerbating poverty and unemployment rates. The lack of access to basic services, such as healthcare and education, further marginalized vulnerable populations, including women, children, and the elderly.

Despite the initial intentions to restore democracy, the intervention failed to address the underlying socio-political issues that perpetuated human rights abuses in Haiti. The lack of comprehensive reforms and the failure to hold perpetrators accountable for past crimes undermined the prospects of lasting change. This subchapter explores the long-term consequences of Operation Uphold Democracy on Haiti's political stability and democratic institutions, highlighting the challenges that persist in the aftermath of the intervention.

By analyzing the impact on human rights and civil liberties, historians gain a comprehensive understanding of the complexities surrounding Operation Uphold Democracy. This subchapter sheds light on the nuances of the intervention, providing a critical perspective on its success or failure in achieving its objectives. It also highlights the importance of considering the experiences and perspectives of Haitian civilians, whose voices are often marginalized in historical narratives. Overall, this subchapter serves as a vital resource for historians seeking a comprehensive analysis of the intervention's impact on human rights and civil liberties in Haiti.

The Rebuilding of Trust and Social Cohesion in Post-Intervention Haiti

After the conclusion of Operation Uphold Democracy, Haiti faced the daunting task of rebuilding trust and social cohesion among its population. The U.S.-led intervention had aimed to restore democracy and stability to the country, but its success in achieving these objectives was debatable. As historians, it is crucial to examine the aftermath of the intervention and assess its impact on Haitian society.

Prior to the intervention, Haiti had a tumultuous political history, marked by authoritarian rule, corruption, and human rights abuses. Operation Uphold Democracy sought to address these issues by removing the military regime and installing a democratic government. However, the transition to democracy proved challenging, and the lack of trust between the population and the newly established authorities was evident.

Rebuilding trust in post-intervention Haiti required addressing the grievances and concerns of the Haitian people. The intervention had brought about significant changes, but the impact on the economy and society was mixed. While some sectors experienced growth and development, others faced challenges, including unemployment, poverty, and limited access to basic services. These issues further strained social cohesion and trust.

The United Nations played a crucial role in the post-intervention phase by providing assistance and support for Haiti's reconstruction efforts. The international community rallied behind Haiti, providing financial aid and technical assistance to help rebuild infrastructure, improve healthcare, and promote education. This support aimed to address the underlying social and economic disparities that had contributed to the political instability in the country.

However, the success of these efforts in rebuilding trust and social cohesion was limited. Haitian civilians, who had endured years of political turmoil and economic hardship, remained skeptical of the promises made by the new government and the international community. The experiences and perspectives of Haitian civilians during and after the intervention revealed a deep-seated distrust and disillusionment with the political process.

The media coverage and public perception of the intervention, both domestically and internationally, also played a significant role in shaping the rebuilding process. The portrayal of the intervention as a foreign imposition and the questioning of its motives further eroded trust among the Haitian population.

The long-term consequences and legacy of Operation Uphold Democracy on Haiti's political stability and democratic institutions were complex. While the intervention succeeded in restoring democracy, it failed to address the underlying social and economic issues that plagued the country. The lack of trust and social cohesion remained significant challenges, hindering Haiti's progress towards political stability and sustainable development.

In conclusion, the rebuilding of trust and social cohesion in post-intervention Haiti was a complex and challenging process. The intervention had brought about significant changes, but its impact on the population's trust in the government and social cohesion was limited. Addressing the underlying social and economic disparities, improving governance, and fostering inclusive dialogue were crucial for rebuilding trust and social cohesion in post-intervention Haiti.

The Long-term Psychological and Emotional Effects on Haitian Civilians

Operation Uphold Democracy, the 1994 U.S.-led multinational military intervention in Haiti, had far-reaching consequences on the Haitian society, economy, and political stability. While the focus of discussions often centers around the military strategy, political implications, and humanitarian aspects of the intervention, it is crucial to acknowledge the long-term psychological and emotional effects on Haitian civilians.

The traumatic experiences endured by Haitian civilians during and after Operation Uphold Democracy left a lasting impact on their mental well-being. The violence, disruption of daily life, and loss of loved ones caused immense psychological distress, leading to high rates of post-traumatic stress disorder (PTSD) and other mental health issues. The constant fear and uncertainty, coupled with the loss of trust in institutions, shattered the sense of security and stability among the population.

Moreover, the intervention exacerbated existing social divisions and deepened the mistrust between different communities. The military strategy employed during Operation Uphold Democracy, including house-to-house searches and arrests, created a hostile environment that further strained relationships within Haitian society. This division and mistrust continue to haunt the country, hindering reconciliation and long-term stability.

The psychological and emotional toll on Haitian civilians also extended to the economic sphere. The disruption caused by the intervention resulted in a decline in economic activity, loss of livelihoods, and increased poverty rates. These socio-economic factors, combined with the psychological trauma, created a vicious cycle of despair and hopelessness among the population.

The long-term consequences of Operation Uphold Democracy on Haiti's democratic institutions cannot be understated. The intervention disrupted the already fragile political landscape, leaving a power vacuum that enabled subsequent political instability. The erosion of trust in democratic processes, combined with the trauma experienced by the population, hindered the development of a strong and stable democracy in Haiti.

To fully understand the impact of Operation Uphold Democracy, it is crucial for historians to delve into the long-term psychological and emotional effects on Haitian civilians. By exploring the trauma experienced by the population, we gain a deeper understanding of the complexities and challenges faced by Haiti in its path towards political stability and democratic governance. Only by addressing these psychological wounds can Haiti truly heal and rebuild its society, economy, and political institutions.

Chapter 9: The Assessment of the Success or Failure of Operation Uphold Democracy in Achieving its Objectives

Evaluating the Achievement of the Stated Objectives

In this subchapter, we will evaluate the success or failure of Operation Uphold Democracy in achieving its objectives. As historians, it is crucial to critically analyze the outcomes of this 1994 U.S.-led multinational military intervention in Haiti. By examining the stated objectives and their impact, we can gain a comprehensive understanding of the operation's effectiveness and its long-term consequences on Haiti's political stability and democratic institutions.

Operation Uphold Democracy aimed to restore democracy and stability in Haiti by removing the military regime of General Raoul Cédras and reinstating Jean-Bertrand Aristide as the democratically elected President. One of the primary objectives was to establish a secure environment where Haitians could freely express their political opinions. However, it is important to assess whether this objective was achieved or if political instability persisted post-intervention.

Additionally, Operation Uphold Democracy sought to address the humanitarian crisis in Haiti. The relief efforts and aid distribution were essential aspects of the intervention. By evaluating the effectiveness of these efforts, we can determine whether they successfully alleviated the suffering of Haitian civilians during and after the operation.

Another crucial aspect to consider is the impact of Operation Uphold Democracy on Haitian society and economy. Did the intervention lead to economic growth and improved social conditions, or did it exacerbate existing challenges? By examining the data, we can assess whether the operation contributed to the long-term development of Haiti or if it had adverse effects on the country.

Furthermore, it is vital to explore the international response and diplomatic implications of the intervention. How did other nations perceive and react to Operation Uphold Democracy? Did it strengthen or strain diplomatic relations between Haiti and other countries? Understanding these aspects will provide insights into the broader geopolitical consequences of the intervention.

Lastly, we must examine the media coverage and public perception of the intervention. How did the media portray Operation Uphold Democracy, both domestically and internationally? Did public opinion shape the narrative surrounding the operation's success or failure? Evaluating these factors will help us understand the role of public perception in shaping historical narratives.

By carefully evaluating the achievement of the stated objectives, we can gain a comprehensive understanding of the success or failure of Operation Uphold Democracy. This assessment will shed light on the long-term consequences and legacy of the intervention on Haiti's political stability and democratic institutions. Through a critical analysis of these factors, historians can contribute to a nuanced understanding of this significant historical event.

The Impact on Political Stability and Security in Haiti

In the subchapter titled "The Impact on Political Stability and Security in Haiti," we delve into the profound effects of Operation Uphold Democracy on Haiti's political landscape and the country's overall security. This subchapter aims to provide historians with a comprehensive understanding of the consequences of the 1994 U.S.-led multinational military intervention in Haiti.

Before delving into the impact of Operation Uphold Democracy, it is essential to grasp the political history of Haiti before and after the U.S.-led intervention. This historical context sets the stage for analyzing the intervention's influence on political stability and security. By exploring the role of the United Nations in Operation Uphold Democracy, we gain insight into the international community's involvement and its implications for Haiti's political future.

Operation Uphold Democracy not only aimed to stabilize Haiti but also sought to address the country's economic challenges. Therefore, this subchapter examines the intervention's impact on Haitian society and economy, highlighting the changes brought about by the international community's efforts.

Furthermore, the subchapter explores the diplomatic implications of Operation Uphold Democracy, analyzing the international response to the intervention and its consequences for Haiti's relations with other nations. Additionally, the military strategy and tactics employed during the operation are examined, shedding light on the military's role in achieving political stability and security.

As historians, it is crucial to consider the humanitarian aspects of Operation Uphold Democracy. This subchapter delves into the relief efforts and aid distribution, evaluating the effectiveness of these initiatives and their impact on the Haitian population.

To provide a comprehensive perspective, the experiences and perspectives of Haitian civilians during and after the intervention are explored. This subchapter aims to uncover the voices of the Haitian people, capturing their narratives and opinions on the intervention.

Ultimately, historians must assess the success or failure of Operation Uphold Democracy in achieving its objectives. By critically evaluating the operation's outcomes, this subchapter offers a nuanced understanding of the intervention's impact on political stability and security in Haiti.

The media coverage and public perception of the intervention, both domestically and internationally, are also examined, providing insight into how Operation Uphold Democracy was portrayed and understood by different audiences.

Finally, this subchapter delves into the long-term consequences and legacy of Operation Uphold Democracy on Haiti's political stability and democratic institutions. By analyzing the lasting effects of the intervention, historians can draw conclusions about its overall impact on Haiti's political trajectory.

In conclusion, the subchapter "The Impact on Political Stability and Security in Haiti" provides historians with a comprehensive analysis of the consequences of Operation Uphold Democracy. By examining various aspects, from political history to military strategy, humanitarian efforts to public perception, this subchapter offers invaluable insights into the long-lasting effects of the intervention on Haiti's political stability and security.

The Effects on Democratization and Governance in Haiti

Haiti, a small Caribbean nation with a tumultuous political history, experienced a significant turning point in its democratization and governance through Operation Uphold Democracy. This subchapter delves into the profound effects of this U.S.-led multinational military intervention on Haiti's political landscape and democratic institutions.

Prior to the intervention, Haiti had been plagued by political instability, authoritarian rule, and widespread corruption. Operation Uphold Democracy aimed to restore democracy and stability, ensuring the protection of human rights and the establishment of a functioning government. The intervention successfully removed the military junta led by General Raoul Cédras and restored President Jean-Bertrand Aristide to power, who had been democratically elected in 1990.

The impact of Operation Uphold Democracy on Haitian society and economy cannot be understated. The intervention brought about an immediate sense of hope and optimism among the Haitian population, who had long endured poverty and social inequality. With the return of Aristide, the government initiated various reforms to address these issues, including the promotion of education, healthcare, and economic development.

The United Nations played a crucial role in Operation Uphold Democracy, providing support in maintaining security, facilitating the return of Aristide, and overseeing the organization of free and fair elections. Their presence helped to rebuild trust in the government and strengthen democratic institutions, contributing to the long-term stability of Haiti.

However, the intervention also had its challenges. The military strategy and tactics employed during Operation Uphold Democracy faced criticism for their heavy-handed approach, resulting in civilian casualties and property damage. Additionally, relief efforts and aid distribution faced logistical difficulties, hindering the immediate recovery of the Haitian society.

The success or failure of Operation Uphold Democracy in achieving its objectives remains a subject of debate among historians. While the intervention succeeded in restoring democracy and initiating reforms, it did not entirely eradicate corruption and poverty. Nevertheless, it set a precedent for future democratic transitions and established a foundation for Haiti's political stability.

The media coverage and public perception of the intervention, both domestically and internationally, played a significant role in shaping the narrative around Operation Uphold Democracy. The portrayal of the intervention as a humanitarian effort had a positive impact on public opinion, both in Haiti and abroad.

Ultimately, the long-term consequences and legacy of Operation Uphold Democracy on Haiti's political stability and democratic institutions are evident. The intervention paved the way for subsequent democratic elections and contributed to the strengthening of Haiti's democratic processes. However, challenges remain, and ongoing efforts are required to address the underlying socio-economic issues and consolidate democratic governance in Haiti.

The Lessons Learned from Operation Uphold Democracy

Operation Uphold Democracy, the 1994 U.S.-led multinational military intervention in Haiti, holds great historical significance in the political history of Haiti. This subchapter aims to delve into the valuable lessons learned from this operation, providing insights for historians and those interested in the various niches surrounding Operation Uphold Democracy.

One crucial lesson learned from this intervention is the importance of understanding the political history of Haiti before and after the U.S.-led intervention. Examining the tumultuous past of Haiti, characterized by political instability and human rights abuses, helps contextualize the motivations behind Operation Uphold Democracy and its subsequent impact on the country.

Another lesson to be gleaned is the role of the United Nations in Operation Uphold Democracy. This intervention marked one of the early instances of UN involvement in peacekeeping operations, highlighting the evolving nature of international cooperation in maintaining global stability.

Furthermore, analyzing the impact of Operation Uphold Democracy on Haitian society and economy is crucial. Understanding how the intervention affected the lives of ordinary Haitian citizens and the economic landscape of the country provides key insights into the humanitarian aspects of the intervention, including relief efforts and aid distribution.

The international response and diplomatic implications of the intervention also deserve attention. Exploring how different nations and international organizations reacted to Operation Uphold Democracy sheds light on the complexities of international relations and the role of diplomacy in resolving conflicts.

Additionally, the military strategy and tactics employed during Operation Uphold Democracy offer valuable lessons in the realm of military operations. Studying the effectiveness of these strategies can help inform future military interventions.

Examining the experiences and perspectives of Haitian civilians during and after Operation Uphold Democracy provides a crucial human element to the analysis. Capturing their voices and understanding their lived experiences can help shape a more comprehensive understanding of the intervention's impact.

Evaluating the success or failure of Operation Uphold Democracy in achieving its objectives is essential for assessing the effectiveness of such interventions. This assessment should take into account both the immediate outcomes and the long-term consequences on Haiti's political stability and democratic institutions.

Finally, exploring the media coverage and public perception of the intervention, both domestically and internationally, can shed light on the role of media in shaping public opinion and influencing policy decisions.

In conclusion, the lessons learned from Operation Uphold Democracy provide valuable insights into the complexities of military interventions, international cooperation, and the impact of such interventions on the target country. By examining the various niches surrounding Operation Uphold Democracy, historians and interested readers can gain a comprehensive understanding of this historical event and its lasting legacy on Haiti.

Chapter 10: The Media Coverage and Public Perception of the Intervention, both Domestically and Internationally

The Role of Media in Shaping the Narrative of Operation Uphold Democracy

Throughout history, the media has played a significant role in shaping public perception and understanding of major events. Operation Uphold Democracy, the 1994 U.S.-led multinational military intervention in Haiti, was no exception. The media's coverage of this operation had far-reaching implications for both domestic and international audiences, making it a crucial aspect to consider when evaluating the intervention's overall success or failure.

From the onset of Operation Uphold Democracy, the media played a pivotal role in disseminating information about the mission's objectives, the military strategy employed, and the humanitarian aspects of the intervention. The media's coverage allowed historians and experts to gain insight into the decision-making process and the rationale behind the intervention. It also provided a platform for different perspectives to be presented, allowing for a more comprehensive understanding of the complex issues at hand.

The media's coverage of Operation Uphold Democracy also had a profound impact on Haitian society and the international community. Through their reporting, journalists brought the plight of Haitian civilians to the forefront, shedding light on the humanitarian crisis and the need for relief efforts. This coverage not only influenced public opinion but also played a crucial role in mobilizing international support and aid for Haiti.

Furthermore, the media's portrayal of the intervention had diplomatic implications, shaping how other nations perceived and responded to Operation Uphold Democracy. The media coverage influenced the international community's stance on the intervention, either garnering support or sparking criticism. This, in turn, had implications for the long-term consequences and legacy of Operation Uphold Democracy, particularly in relation to Haiti's political stability and democratic institutions.

It is essential for historians and those interested in Operation Uphold Democracy to critically examine the media coverage of the intervention. By analyzing the narratives presented, historians can gain a deeper understanding of the context in which the intervention took place and the various factors that influenced its outcome. This analysis can help historians assess the success or failure of Operation Uphold Democracy in achieving its objectives and evaluate its impact on Haitian society and economy.

In conclusion, the role of the media in shaping the narrative of Operation Uphold Democracy cannot be overstated. Historians and those interested in this intervention must consider the media coverage and public perception to gain a comprehensive understanding of the operation's complexities, diplomatic implications, and long-term consequences. By doing so, they can paint a more accurate and nuanced picture of Operation Uphold Democracy and its significance in both Haitian and international history.

The Coverage and Reporting of Human Rights Violations and Abuses

In the subchapter titled "The Coverage and Reporting of Human Rights Violations and Abuses," we delve into one of the most critical aspects of Operation Uphold Democracy: the documentation and dissemination of human rights violations and abuses. The information presented in this chapter is of particular interest to historians and those interested in understanding the multifaceted impact of this U.S.-led multinational military intervention in Haiti.

Operation Uphold Democracy was not only aimed at restoring democratic governance in Haiti but also at ensuring the protection and promotion of human rights. As such, it is crucial to examine how these violations and abuses were covered and reported during and after the intervention.

The media played a pivotal role in shaping public perception of Operation Uphold Democracy. Domestically and internationally, journalists were tasked with providing accurate and unbiased coverage of the unfolding events. However, it is important to acknowledge that the media's access to certain areas and information may have been limited, leading to potential gaps in reporting.

This subchapter explores the challenges faced by journalists in their efforts to report on human rights violations and abuses. It examines how their reporting influenced public opinion, both within Haiti and abroad, and how it shaped the international response to the intervention.

Additionally, this subchapter delves into the experiences and perspectives of Haitian civilians during and after Operation Uphold Democracy. By examining their accounts, historians gain invaluable insights into the impact of human rights violations and abuses on the Haitian society and economy.

Moreover, this subchapter analyzes the long-term consequences and legacy of Operation Uphold Democracy on Haiti's political stability and democratic institutions. By examining the media coverage and public perception of the intervention, historians gain a comprehensive understanding of how the events were remembered and interpreted over time.

In conclusion, "The Coverage and Reporting of Human Rights Violations and Abuses" subchapter sheds light on the critical role of media in documenting and disseminating information about Operation Uphold Democracy. By examining the media coverage, public perception, and long-term consequences, historians can assess the success or failure of the intervention in achieving its objectives and evaluate its impact on Haiti's political stability and democratic institutions.

The Domestic and International Public Opinions on the Intervention

One of the crucial aspects to consider when analyzing Operation Uphold Democracy is the domestic and international public opinions on the intervention. Understanding how the intervention was perceived by different audiences provides valuable insights into the broader impact and legacy of the operation.

Domestically, the initial reaction to the U.S.-led intervention in Haiti was mixed. While some segments of the population welcomed the intervention as a means to restore stability and democracy, others viewed it as an infringement on Haitian sovereignty. Critics argued that the intervention was driven by self-interest rather than a genuine concern for the welfare of the Haitian people. These divergent opinions led to debates and protests within Haiti, highlighting the complex nature of public sentiment towards the intervention.

Internationally, the intervention received varying degrees of support and criticism. Many countries in the Western Hemisphere, particularly those in the Caribbean and Latin America, expressed their approval for the intervention. They saw it as a necessary step to prevent a humanitarian crisis and protect regional stability. However, some nations, such as Cuba and Venezuela, vehemently opposed the intervention, viewing it as an imperialistic act by the United States.

The international community at large also held different views on the intervention. While some countries endorsed the military action, others questioned its legitimacy, arguing that it set a dangerous precedent for intervention in the internal affairs of sovereign states. The United Nations played a significant role in shaping international public opinion through its involvement in the operation, with the Security Council approving the deployment of a multinational force.

Media coverage played a crucial role in shaping public opinion both domestically and internationally. The way the intervention was portrayed in the media influenced how it was perceived by different audiences. Some media outlets supported the intervention, emphasizing its humanitarian objectives and the need for stability in Haiti. However, others criticized the intervention, questioning its effectiveness and highlighting the negative consequences for the Haitian population.

Understanding the domestic and international public opinions on the intervention is essential for historians studying Operation Uphold Democracy. It provides valuable insights into the complexities of the intervention and its broader impact on Haiti's political stability and democratic institutions. By analyzing the diverse perspectives and reactions to the intervention, historians can assess the success or failure of Operation Uphold Democracy in achieving its objectives and evaluate its long-term consequences on Haitian society and economy.

The Influence of Media on Public Perception and Support for the Intervention

The media plays a crucial role in shaping public opinion and perception of significant events, and Operation Uphold Democracy in Haiti was no exception. The coverage of the intervention by the media had a profound impact on the public's understanding and support for the U.S.-led multinational military intervention.

Media coverage of the intervention was extensive, both domestically and internationally. Journalists from various news outlets provided live updates, images, and interviews, giving the public a front-row seat to the unfolding events in Haiti. This comprehensive coverage allowed people to witness the challenges faced by the Haitian people and the efforts made by the international community to restore stability and democracy.

The media's portrayal of the intervention heavily influenced public perception. Initially, the coverage focused on the dire humanitarian situation in Haiti, with images of violence, poverty, and political instability dominating the headlines. These portrayals raised awareness and garnered sympathy for the Haitian people, which consequently increased public support for the intervention.

As the intervention progressed, media coverage shifted its focus to the successes and failures of the mission. Journalists reported on the progress made in restoring order, delivering aid, and rebuilding Haiti's infrastructure. However, they also highlighted the challenges faced by the multinational forces, such as resistance from armed factions and the slow pace of progress. These reports shaped public perception of the intervention as both a necessary and complex undertaking.

The media's coverage also influenced international support for the intervention. Images of Haitian civilians suffering from violence and poverty were broadcasted globally, leading to an outpouring of support from various countries. The media played a crucial role in disseminating information about the intervention's objectives and the need for international assistance.

However, the media's coverage was not without criticism. Some argued that the media sensationalized certain aspects of the intervention, focusing on negative incidents, and failing to provide a balanced perspective. Others believed that the media's coverage failed to adequately highlight the long-term consequences and legacy of Operation Uphold Democracy on Haiti's political stability and democratic institutions.

In conclusion, the media's coverage of Operation Uphold Democracy significantly influenced public perception and support for the intervention. Its comprehensive reporting allowed the public to witness the challenges faced by the Haitian people and the efforts made by the international community. However, the media's portrayal was not without flaws, and some aspects of the intervention were sensationalized or overlooked. Despite this, the media played a crucial role in shaping public opinion and awareness of the intervention's objectives and impact.

Chapter 11: The Long-term Consequences and Legacy of Operation Uphold Democracy on Haiti's Political Stability and Democratic Institutions

The Impact on Haiti's Democratic Institutions and Governance

In examining the impact of Operation Uphold Democracy on Haiti's democratic institutions and governance, it is essential to consider the political history of Haiti both before and after the U.S.-led intervention. Prior to Operation Uphold Democracy, Haiti had experienced decades of political instability, corruption, and authoritarian rule. The intervention aimed to restore democracy, strengthen institutions, and promote good governance.

Operation Uphold Democracy, a 1994 U.S.-led multinational military intervention in Haiti, played a crucial role in shaping the nation's democratic trajectory. The United Nations also played a significant part in supporting and overseeing the operation, ensuring the establishment of democratic institutions and the rule of law.

The impact of the intervention on Haitian society and the economy cannot be overstated. The operation brought stability to a nation torn apart by violence and political unrest. It paved the way for economic growth and development, attracting foreign investment and aid. Through relief efforts and aid distribution, the intervention provided much-needed support to the Haitian people, improving living conditions and reducing poverty levels.

The experiences and perspectives of Haitian civilians during and after Operation Uphold Democracy were diverse. For many, the intervention offered hope for a better future, while others remained skeptical of foreign involvement and questioned the sustainability of democratic institutions. Nevertheless, the intervention provided a platform for the citizens to participate in the democratic process, empowering them to shape their own destiny.

Assessing the success or failure of Operation Uphold Democracy in achieving its objectives is a complex task. While the intervention successfully restored democratic governance and stability in the short term, long-term consequences and legacy must also be considered. The intervention did not completely eradicate corruption or address the underlying socio-economic challenges facing Haiti, leaving the nation vulnerable to future political instability.

The media coverage and public perception of the intervention, both domestically and internationally, have varied. While some praised the operation as a necessary step towards democracy, others criticized it as an example of foreign interventionism. Understanding these different perspectives is crucial in unraveling the complexities of Operation Uphold Democracy.

Ultimately, the long-term consequences and legacy of Operation Uphold Democracy on Haiti's political stability and democratic institutions are still unfolding. While the intervention made significant strides in restoring democracy and fostering economic growth, the nation continues to face challenges. To fully grasp the impact of Operation Uphold Democracy, historians must analyze the events leading up to the intervention, the intervention itself, and the subsequent developments in Haiti's political landscape.

The Challenges in Sustaining Political Stability in Post-Intervention Haiti

The 1994 U.S.-led multinational military intervention in Haiti, known as Operation Uphold Democracy, aimed to restore democratic governance, political stability, and economic prosperity to the country. While the intervention initially achieved its objectives, sustaining political stability in post-intervention Haiti has proven to be a significant challenge.

One of the main challenges in sustaining political stability in post-intervention Haiti is the political history of the country both before and after the U.S.-led intervention. Haiti has a long history of political instability, characterized by coups, corruption, and weak institutions. These challenges persisted even after the intervention, with political leaders struggling to establish effective governance structures and maintain public trust.

The role of the United Nations (UN) in Operation Uphold Democracy was crucial in ensuring political stability. However, the UN's presence in Haiti has faced its own set of challenges, including limited resources and the need to balance the interests of various stakeholders. Additionally, the impact of Operation Uphold Democracy on Haitian society and economy has been mixed, with some sectors experiencing positive changes while others continue to struggle.

The international response and diplomatic implications of the intervention have also posed challenges to sustaining political stability in Haiti. While the intervention was generally well-received internationally, there have been debates and criticisms regarding the long-term consequences and effectiveness of the intervention. These debates have influenced international support and aid to Haiti, which has had implications for the country's political stability.

The experiences and perspectives of Haitian civilians during and after Operation Uphold Democracy are crucial in understanding the challenges of sustaining political stability. Many Haitians have faced socio-economic hardships and have expressed frustration with the slow pace of progress. Addressing these concerns and ensuring the inclusion of all segments of society is vital for sustaining political stability.

The media coverage and public perception of the intervention, both domestically and internationally, have also impacted efforts to sustain political stability. Media narratives and public opinion can shape policy decisions and international support, making it imperative to address any negative perceptions and provide accurate information about the progress made in Haiti.

The long-term consequences and legacy of Operation Uphold Democracy on Haiti's political stability and democratic institutions are still unfolding. It is essential to continuously evaluate the impact of the intervention and make necessary adjustments to address the challenges that arise. This requires ongoing commitment from both the international community and the Haitian government to prioritize political stability and democratic governance.

In conclusion, sustaining political stability in post-intervention Haiti has proven to be a complex and challenging task. Addressing the historical context, the role of the UN, the impact on society and the economy, the international response, the experiences of Haitian civilians, the media coverage, and the long-term consequences are all crucial for understanding and overcoming these challenges. By acknowledging these obstacles and working together, historians can contribute to a comprehensive understanding of the complexities involved in sustaining political stability in post-intervention Haiti.

The Role of International Assistance in Rebuilding Haiti's Institutions

After the 1994 U.S.-led multinational military intervention in Haiti, known as Operation Uphold Democracy, the focus shifted to rebuilding Haiti's institutions and restoring stability to the country. International assistance played a crucial role in this process, providing the necessary resources and expertise to help Haiti transition towards a more democratic and prosperous future.

One of the key areas where international assistance was instrumental was in the rebuilding of Haiti's political institutions. The intervention aimed to establish a functioning democracy, and this required the establishment of democratic institutions such as a new constitution, a reformed judiciary, and a professional police force. International actors, including the United Nations, played a vital role in providing technical assistance and financial support to strengthen these institutions. They helped train Haitian officials, provided electoral support, and facilitated the drafting of a new constitution that guaranteed human rights and democratic principles.

Furthermore, international assistance was crucial in rebuilding Haiti's economy, which had been severely impacted by years of political instability and economic mismanagement. Donor countries and international organizations provided financial aid, investment, and technical expertise to help stimulate economic growth, create jobs, and alleviate poverty. These efforts included infrastructure development, agricultural programs, and support for small businesses. The goal was to create a sustainable economy that would provide opportunities for Haitians and reduce their dependence on foreign aid.

In addition to political and economic reconstruction, international assistance played a crucial role in addressing the humanitarian needs of the Haitian people. The intervention had brought a degree of stability to the country, but it also revealed the extent of the humanitarian crisis. International organizations, non-governmental organizations, and donor countries stepped in to provide emergency relief, including food, water, medical care, and shelter. They also focused on long-term development projects to improve access to education, healthcare, and clean water.

The role of international assistance in rebuilding Haiti's institutions cannot be underestimated. It provided the necessary resources, expertise, and support to help Haiti transition towards a more stable and prosperous future. However, it is important to recognize that the process of rebuilding institutions is complex and takes time. Challenges and setbacks were encountered along the way, and it is important for historians to critically assess the impact of international assistance in achieving its objectives. Nonetheless, it is clear that without international assistance, the task of rebuilding Haiti's institutions would have been much more challenging, if not impossible.

Assessing the Legacy of Operation Uphold Democracy on Haiti's Political Future

Operation Uphold Democracy, the 1994 U.S.-led multinational military intervention in Haiti, had a profound impact on the country's political future. This subchapter aims to assess the long-term consequences and legacy of this operation on Haiti's political stability and democratic institutions.

Before delving into the legacy of Operation Uphold Democracy, it is essential to understand the political history of Haiti before and after the U.S.-led intervention. From the tumultuous period of dictatorship under the Duvalier regime to the subsequent cycles of political instability, Haiti faced numerous challenges in establishing a democratic system. Operation Uphold Democracy aimed to restore democracy and stability to Haiti, but its success in achieving this objective is still a subject of debate among historians.

One significant aspect to consider is the role of the United Nations in Operation Uphold Democracy. The UN played a crucial role in supporting the intervention and helping with the transition to democracy. However, the effectiveness of the UN's involvement in achieving long-term political stability in Haiti remains a point of contention.

Operation Uphold Democracy also had a significant impact on Haitian society and economy. While it successfully restored some semblance of stability, the intervention failed to address the underlying socio-economic issues that plagued the country. The subchapter will explore the impact of the operation on Haitian society, including the relief efforts and aid distribution, and analyze how these efforts shaped the country's social fabric.

Additionally, the international response and diplomatic implications of the intervention are crucial in understanding its legacy. The subchapter will examine the reactions and perspectives of various countries and international organizations towards Operation Uphold Democracy, shedding light on the intervention's broader implications.

Furthermore, the assessment of the success or failure of Operation Uphold Democracy in achieving its objectives is a critical aspect to explore. By examining the military strategy and tactics employed during the operation, the subchapter will evaluate whether the intervention achieved its intended goals.

The experiences and perspectives of Haitian civilians during and after Operation Uphold Democracy are also vital in understanding its legacy. By considering their voices, the subchapter will provide a comprehensive analysis of how the intervention affected the Haitian population.

The media coverage and public perception of the intervention, both domestically and internationally, will be examined to gain insights into how Operation Uphold Democracy was portrayed and understood.

Ultimately, this subchapter aims to provide a comprehensive assessment of the legacy of Operation Uphold Democracy on Haiti's political stability and democratic institutions. By analyzing various aspects such as the international response, military strategy, humanitarian efforts, and the experiences of Haitian civilians, historians can gain a nuanced understanding of the long-term consequences of this intervention.

Epilogue: Reflections on Operation Uphold Democracy and Its Historical Significance

As historians, we have the unique privilege of analyzing events in their historical context and evaluating their significance. In this epilogue, we reflect on Operation Uphold Democracy, the 1994 U.S.-led multinational military intervention in Haiti, and delve into its historical importance.

Operation Uphold Democracy marked a crucial turning point in the political history of Haiti. Before this intervention, Haiti had been plagued by political instability, corruption, and human rights abuses. The U.S.-led intervention aimed to restore democracy, promote stability, and protect the rights of Haitian civilians. We must assess the extent to which these objectives were achieved and the long-term consequences for Haiti's political landscape.

The United Nations played a pivotal role in Operation Uphold Democracy, providing international legitimacy and support. We analyze the UN's involvement and examine its impact on the success of the intervention.

Furthermore, we explore the multifaceted impact of Operation Uphold Democracy on Haitian society and economy. Did the intervention succeed in improving the lives of ordinary Haitians, or did it exacerbate existing socio-economic disparities? We delve into the humanitarian aspects of the intervention, including relief efforts and aid distribution, to understand its impact on the lives of Haitian civilians.

Moreover, the international response and diplomatic implications of the intervention cannot be overlooked. We examine the reactions of other nations and assess the long-term implications for Haiti's foreign relations.

In our analysis, we shed light on the military strategy and tactics employed during Operation Uphold Democracy. Did these approaches effectively achieve the intended objectives, or were there unintended consequences? By critically evaluating the military aspects, we gain a comprehensive understanding of the intervention's execution.

A crucial aspect of any historical event is the perspective of those directly affected. We explore the experiences and perspectives of Haitian civilians during and after Operation Uphold Democracy, giving voice to their stories and evaluating the impact of the intervention on their lives.

We also delve into the media coverage and public perception of the intervention, both domestically and internationally. How did the media shape public opinion, and how did this influence the trajectory of the intervention? By analyzing the media's role, we gain insight into the broader public discourse surrounding Operation Uphold Democracy.

Lastly, we assess the overall success or failure of Operation Uphold Democracy in achieving its objectives. By critically evaluating the intervention's outcomes, we can draw valuable lessons and contribute to the ongoing debate surrounding its efficacy.

In conclusion, Operation Uphold Democracy left a lasting legacy on Haiti's political stability and democratic institutions. By reflecting on its historical significance, we strive to deepen our understanding of this

pivotal intervention and its broader implications for the region and
beyond.

Milton Keynes UK
Ingram Content Group UK Ltd.
UKHW011938010124
435297UK00001B/117

9 798223 610199